This anthology is dedicated
to the memory of
Jane Eve Wilheit,
who remained a member
and avid supporter of
Northeast Georgia Writers
from the beginning in 1973.

She truly believed in the beauty, power and
value of the written word, and we are
grateful for her inspiration.

"Gainesville has been blessed to have had Jane Eve Wilheit live among us and contribute so much of her talent and personality. She was a true friend and we will thoroughly miss her."

—Lessie Smithgall

... Written about her fellow charter member of
Northeast Georgia Writers.

OUR JOURNEY

NORTHEAST GEORGIA WRITERS

2007 ANTHOLOGY

Published by the Northeast Georgia Writers

TABLE OF CONTENTS

PREPARING FOR THE JOURNEY

Hey, Paddle!	Harris	2
My Day's Exchange	Emerson	4
Grace So Amazing	Harris	5
In Praise of Imperfection	Hopkins	7
Morning Hymn	Harris-Mallinson	8
Entering The Ark/Shekinah Fire	Harris-Mallinson	9
America, Standing Tall	Stargel	12
Memories Reveal Turning Point Moments	Whitten	13
A Penny Saved	Baumgardner	14
What Christmas Means to Me	Brady	15
A Poet's Heart	Emerson	16
The Pearl Inside	Ramsey	17
Paradox	Wildman	18
The Tower of Babel	Woodcock	18
Longings of a Nonentity	Baumgardner	20
Love	Emerson	21

PLACES ON THE JOURNEY

The Summertime Lake Jamboree	Holmes	24
Valentine's Day, Number 65	Ramsey	25
You are Never Too Old for a Hike in the Mountains of Beautiful North Georgia	Clark	26
Within the Silence	Harris-Mallinson	28
God's Beautiful Summer Surprise	Marlow	29
Our Woodland Home	Martin	31
My Father's Spare Change	Clark	33
What Do They Say?	Harper	34
A Road Home	Harper	35
Sojourn of My Soul	Wildman	36
My Yard and Container Combo Experience	Whitten	37
Death of a Village	Stargel	39
A Magical Hour	McConnon	41
Standing Strong	Brady	42

TABLE OF CONTENTS

PEOPLE ON THE JOURNEY

The Impact of a Fictional Maria	Harris	44
Cousin Luther	Caples	45
What is a Mentor?	Brady	46
My First Valentine	Marlow	46
Yuhlon	Caples	47
April Paradox	Hopkins	49
The Birder	Paget	50
Adventure vs. Wedding Bells	Ellett	51
A Special Day Just for Dad	Ellett	52
Daddy's Cubbyhole	Ellett	53
A Dose of Humor	Woodcock	56
Driving Lessons	Holmes	57
Evelyn, the Skeleton	Paget	59
In a Pickle	Ramsey	60
The Change-Maker	Caples	61
Lost Dream	Paget	62
Life Without Jurgen	McConnon	63
When I Look at You	Woodcock	64
Requiem for a Matriarch	Hopkins	66

PICTURES ON THE JOURNEY

From the Balcony	Collier	68
The Keeper	Bass	69
Green Street	Bass	69
Pages in a Book	Harper	70
Purple Flowers	Collier	71
The Day My Son Became a Marine	Stargel	72
The Cabin	Wildman	74
Blue Heron	Martin	74
Haven	Martin	75
Honored Woman	Collier	76
Families	Whitten	77
African Market Day	McConnon	79
Talking Hands	Bass	80
Flying High	Holmes	81

Preparing for the Journey

Hey, Paddle!
Laura Leigh Harris

Hey, paddle! It's Sunday, so where shall we go?
Past double-slipped docks? By a beaver's condo?
Little River twists and turns on its course with no sound
'Neath the bridge, through the tree, 'round the Indian mound.
Pour the early spring rains as they start to refill
The red barren banks of the valleys and hills.

Hey, paddle! It's Monday, so where shall we go?
To the park and the tower where the Chattahoochee flows?
Canoes, and kayaks, and boats all the buzz
Break through thick, glazing layers of green pollen fuzz.
The Red Tail Hawk takes its nest inventory,
Then soars late spring air, in all of its glory.

Hey, paddle! It's Tuesday, so where shall we go?
Straight up Wahoo Creek to see deer or a doe?
The hot summer drought makes you say to your daughter,
"Take a dip in the lake; it's like warm bath water!"
Such low water levels sicken people to despair,
When the dam gauge is found to be in sad disrepair.

Hey, paddle! It's Wednesday, so where shall we go?
The days are cooler; do we still need to mow?
The fallish air clashes with warm currents high
As the loud thunder scatters 'cross the gray, sunless sky.
The Chestatee drifts its way down, toward the south,
For there it will rest—by the dam; by the mouth.

Hey, paddle! It's Thursday, so where shall we go?
Are we ready to harvest what we earlier sowed?
The brisk, late fall chill colors leaves, builds a bog;
And the bass boats have trouble getting 'round in the fog.
Fewer boats are seen traveling underneath Brown's Bridge,
Instead moored at their docks; seen from yonder high ridge.

Hey, paddle! It's Friday, so where shall we go?
Winter is with us; do you think it will snow?
The calm surface glistens; no wind is the reason,
As we think on the One who's the King of the season.
Should we float down the creek to dine at *Up the Creek*?
Or, should we just take a nap for the rest of the week?

Hey, paddle! It's Saturday, so where shall we go?
There's still some time left, the sun is aglow.
Late winter renders West Bank cold, dark and lonely;
The water park befriends little birds and squirrels only.
The dam, it sits lifeless; in the warm sun it bakes,
Yearning for people to cross, who love this dear lake.

Hey, paddle! What a constant companion you've been
To my orange-yellow kayak and me; what a friend!
From shore, around bend, to the tip of the pier;
Great adventures we've seen on Lake Sidney Lanier.

2007 *Northeast Georgia Writers*: Third Place, Poetry

MY DAY'S EXCHANGE
Blanche Buchanan Emerson

As I arise in the morning,
this is the beginning of a new day.

The Lord has given me this day,
I can use it as I please.

I can use this day to do good for others,
or I can waste it on foolish things.

What I do with this day is important,
because I am exchanging a day of my life for it.

When tomorrow arrives,
this day will be gone forever.

In its place,
I will have exchanged something for it.

I want it to be,
good and thoughtful deeds for others.

Then I will be happy,
and not regret the price I paid for it.

GRACE SO AMAZING
Laura Leigh Harris

Has life ever hinted at the need for a new direction? Were you willing to change, even if you viewed the current direction as, well—not flawless—but okay? My mid-twenties brought me to an intersection in life where circumstances opened my eyes to much-needed spiritual direction. Thankfully, salvation in Christ placed my feet firmly on a new path, so I moved forward. Reflecting back, now that I am fifty-something, I realize that God knew my future and saw the significance for my alignment with Him. It was God who would provide the courage, strength, and perseverance necessary to undergo a season of long-suffering. If only I would trust Him.

My husband and I started our spiritual journey in a church whose pastor carefully shepherded the sheep in his flock. He served a meaty diet of God's Word from the pulpit, which kept us informed and grounded. I greatly appreciated the pastor's efforts to equip us for the real world, by helping us to recognize and deal with the negative forces that might lead us astray. We desired to stand strong against the wiles of alcoholism and divorce—both of which were familiar. To this day my husband and I view this pastor and his wife as honored, spiritual parents.

During the months following my spiritual rebirth, the pastor preached two messages that impacted my life. In 1 Kings 3, Solomon made known his love for the Lord. When God offered to reward his faithfulness, Solomon asked for a wise and discerning heart. I realized that I had not operated my life in wisdom, and Solomon's prayer became the cry of my heart. Shortly after my prayer, the Lord presented situations in life that increased my faith and sharpened my discernment. In a clear way, I viewed God at work in my life.

On another Sunday, with Ezekiel 47 as the scripture of choice, my attention focused on the water flowing from the temple and the depths of water pooled outside the temple. To me, the pastor's poignant question was, "How deep do you want to go with God?" As he likened the different depths of water to the depth of our relationship with God, my heart felt challenged, especially when the pastor depicted swimming in water so deep that the bottom couldn't be touched. I envisioned myself in that deep water, giving up control of my own life and trusting God with every aspect of my existence. God knew my immediate future and the level of commitment required on my part to finish the race set before me.

The day after making that personal commitment, my mom suffered a debilitating stroke. Massive brain damage left her permanently vegetative, and after two months in the hospital, we moved her to a nursing home for assistance with her daily medical needs. Within six months, not only had I learned to fine-tune my roles as wife, mom, and caregiver, but I also began serving my mom as her legal guardian. Those last two roles continued for the next twenty years, along with the normal roles of wife and parent.

Basking in the blessings that complement marriage, parenthood, serving the Lord in my church, and working full-time, those twenty years with my mom brought some joy. More consuming were the battles, sadness, and disappointments. I almost walked away from my relationship with God at one point, totally frustrated. While carrying this ever-present and heavy burden, I prayed continually for grace and mercy. I questioned the existence of God's grace as my mother continued to suffer physically from negligent care in the nursing homes. In times of extreme disappointment, I puzzled over the true meaning of God's grace.

Two years before my mom's death, I spent quality time reflecting on eighteen years of caregiving and legal guardianship responsibilities. Expressing thanks for my strong faith, along with lasting peace and joy, it finally dawned on me that my early prayers had been answered. *I had been in the deep with God.* My mom's suffering had created the deep waters that allowed God to work in my life. He taught me the importance of wisdom and how to surrender my will. I stood strong in perseverance—not giving up when the going got tough. I learned how to bear enormous loads of responsibility, and how to lay down the load before it became too wearisome.

God's perfect peace became my ally, especially with fierce battles raging instead of ceasing. My frustrations transformed into humility and trust as I discovered how to rest in His timing. I moved forward only when He told me to go. And I learned the power of true forgiveness, which encompasses all aspects of life.

Through it all, I recognized that, no matter how deep and stormy the waters appeared, my head always seemed to stay above the waterline. At times, I thought I could no longer navigate the treacherous seas, yet I never went under or sank. Instead, I stayed afloat as the waves crashed sometimes uncontrollably around me. And when the storms temporarily ceased, I rested in the calm seas with the warmth of the sun on my face.

This is what makes grace so amazing! God was with me the whole time, teaching me and refining my character as He undergirded me in the unfathomable. God's grace was my lifejacket in those deep waters.

2007 *Northeast Georgia Writers*: Third Place, Non-Fiction Article
Originally published in *The Valley Christian Chronicle*, May 2002

IN PRAISE OF IMPERFECTION
Marsha Hopkins

I love to walk along the beach at sunrise
And feel the soft breeze blow across my face.
The cool waves lap in rhythm on my bare feet.
I'm so at peace when I am in that place.

I pick the shells that others would just pass by –
The ones cracked open and not really whole.
I look inside to capture all their wonder.
They bring such joy – they touch my very soul.

I trace the spirals all around the inside,
The heart exposed for anyone to see.
I turn and turn each one around my fingers,
And think how they are really just like me.

I take them home to help me to remember
When life breaks in and tears me all apart,
Things I go through serve so well to polish me
And make more beautiful my inner heart.

If we can learn to love the less than perfect
In ourselves and others along the way;
If we will share our lovely, broken insides,
Then there may be a bright and better day.

2006 *Northeast Georgia Writers*: Song Lyrics Award

MORNING HYMN
Rosemary Harris-Mallinson

Lord, I hear your voice in the morning
  Calling me, calling to me —
    In majestic colors that streak the sky
      with the rising sun,
    In the fragrance of dew-freshened flowers,
      as their day, too is begun,
    In the voices of birds in their leafy homes
      among your majestic trees — all these . . .
Are praising you, Lord, in the morning,
    And so am I!

Then into my soul I go deeper
  To listen and hear Your Song
    That flows into me with Your Music,
      Your beautiful heavenly Music
    From Your flutes with Your chorus of angels,
      From Your harps with a *thousand* strings,
  As I listen, and listen, and listen —
Yes, I'll listen and hear,
    And I'll sing!

Reprinted with permission from
In Search Of The Song, Pathways To Communion, © 2003

MEDITATION
ENTERING THE ARK
Rosemary Harris-Mallinson

Dearly Beloved, you are invited to quiet your mind, to gently breathe — breathe — to begin where life in you begins — with breathing, softly, quietly, steadily, in and out, giving full attention to the most basic of all activities, the simple act of breathing.

As you thus give your attention to your breathing, remember when, as a tiny newborn baby, you took your very first breath, and your next, and your next — gradually, slowly becoming aware of this tiny living breathing temple of energy, that is the same living breathing temple that is still you, filled now with light — that holy Shekinah light of the Spirit of God, that once indwelled the holy Ark of the Covenant — pulsing, breathing, living there, guiding that early nation of Israel through the desert to the Promised Land, a living presence of God who would commune there with his people.

Now vision your body as this same temple of energy, and putting aside all awareness except that of your breathing — which is the first building block of awareness — see yourself now filled with this same holy light, the Christ Light shining in you, through you — out into the world, as you — you who are also a living, breathing extension of the living God, living in a body of glorious energy, which is His sacred holy Temple.

As you continue to breathe in your quiet space, let that space be sanctified, and hear in your mind the words of the poet, Gary Snyder, "Where we breathe, we bow." Feel the energy now, and let your own spirit bow, in awesome wonder.

Let your awareness continue to grown and to remember — remember how energy itself can be transformed in awareness from one type to another, just as the crawling caterpillar will one day become aware that it was really born to be a beautiful butterfly — or as the humble green jacaranda tree will one day burst into luminous flaming lavender, or that the scrawny ugly cygnet duckling will, as it grows, suddenly become aware that it is really a beautiful graceful gliding — swan!

And so as we too, remember — know — that such transformations as these are for the delight of God — the very impulse that inspired the Hindu mystic, Aurobindo, to declare, "We are here for the delight of God."

As we continue to expand our awareness, fulfilling in us the Genesis insight that we are made in the image of God, let your consciousness burst into a bouquet of sheer joy and rapture, touched by the abundant mysterious awesome Spirit within us, this wonderful flaming energy that is God in us.

As in the Hebrew, where the most sacred name for the Divine contained only consonants — the word being too sacred to even pronounce — translates into English as Yahweh — consider the consonants in the sacred word itself called the "tetragramaton."

They are perhaps the softest of consonants there are, which may be transliterated as "yodh," "heh," "waw," and "heh." — be breathed! "yodh," "heh," "waw," "heh." — so is the Divine represented by breath — your breath, breathing softly now in you.

Jesus said, "The Kingdom is with you and shall be in you," and so it is when we become aware of this holy Presence in us.

Robert Frost touched this in his simple little poem, "The Secret Sits" — He wrote: "We dance round and round in a ring and suppose, and the Secret sits in the middle and knows." — another variant of the ancient call to allow our minds to be transformed from our self-made illusions to a remembering of the knowing — a true knowing of the presence of the Christ in us who has always been there, waiting — waiting for us to behold Him — to experience His peace in us — and at the same time, to remember the sacred, holy song we once sang around God's throne, the words of which, if we could only remember them all, would be so beautiful we would want to cry!

So now, as we bring ourselves back from our quiet space where, for these few moments we have mentally bowed, and allowed ourselves to contemplate our inner knowing, I invite you to bring back with you the essence of that holy peace — the peace that is rightfully yours — the peace that can never be taken from you.

Lastly, as a sort of addendum to this meditation, I would like to share with you a poem, which seems to express in poetry, the essence of it all.

SHEKINAH FIRE

"The Lord is in His Holy Temple,"
Habakkuk proclaims, and then,
Let all the earth keep silence
Before Him..."
Those wonder-filled words re-echo and sing
Of majesty, reverence and awe,
In a call to a chaotic weary world that waits
To adore Him.

But this temple is more than mortar and stone
With altars and pageantry.
It's more than windows of colorful glass
And elegant tapestry,
For God's Holy Spirit indwells this space
With the light of His presence, His glory and grace,
Where we've only to open our hearts to know
That this temple we'd reverence is we!

So we'll tabernacle now with the Light
In descanted harmony
As the fragrance and incense of unspoken prayer
Anoints us and sets us free.
While His guiding eternal Shekinah Fire
That fills us and calls us to follow
Is lighting our way into Oneness,
In Communion and Unity.

Yes, Lord, we'll immerse ourselves in Your Light,
Until we become the Essence,
The Radiant Hallowed Presence
Of the Light we have come here to be.
Let it fill us all now, let us joyously share
This Light and this Love with each other,
The Light that will heal us and teach us to sing
Your song in Harmony.

Namasté!

Reprinted by permission from
"In Search Of The Song", Pathways To Communion," © *2003,* pg. 9.

AMERICA, STANDING TALL
Gloria Cassity Stargel

Blessed is the nation whose God is the Lord.
Psalm 33:12a (AMP)

It happened on a cold December night. At *Babyland General® Hospital* in Cleveland, Georgia, of all places! This birthplace of the famous *Cabbage Patch* Kids ® was hosting a promotional event for the U. S. Marine Corps' Annual *Toys for Tots* ®.

Fun activities were in full swing, everywhere a festive atmosphere. Inside the white frame building, youngsters watched with eyes wide as uniformed "nurses" in the *cabbage patch* "delivered" cloth babies.

Outside, where colorful, twinkling lights adorned every accessible tree and shrub, exuberant volunteers manned hotdog stands, popcorn machines, and hot chocolate dispensers, while excited children awaited the arrival of the high school band escorting a horse-drawn wagon bearing Santa Claus!

Singing groups gathered on the makeshift stage under a marquee of bare-limbed oaks, their "Silent Nights" and "Up on the Housetops" wafting along the winter breezes.

Listening to the Toys for Tots Singers, I stood next to our area Marine recruiter. The young sergeant was the *picture* of a proud Marine—shoulders back, chest out. Wearing dress blues, white cover positioned squarely on his head, the sergeant's black shoes were shined so brightly they mirrored the colorful, twinkling lights.

From out of the milling crowd appeared a young man with his daughter—she must have been about five. "Pardon me, Sergeant," he said. "May my little girl have a word with you?"

Appearing somewhat taken aback, the Marine nodded "yes."

Whereupon the child, with great dignity, walked around to face him. Drawing herself up to full height, possibly 2 ½ feet, she fixed her gaze upon the ribbons on his chest, placed her right hand over her heart and, with utmost solemnity, began, "I pledge allegiance to the flag of the United States of America..."

The sergeant quietly shifted position from *At Ease* to *Attention* while, in a clear small voice, the little one recited the Pledge to its conclusion, "one nation, under God, indivisible, with liberty and justice for all."

The Marine's trained-to-be-tough features never flinched. But as a light beam caught his face, I detected something in his eye that wanted to be a tear. I know, because I choked down one myself.

For to that dear child, the young Marine sergeant *was* America. And how fitting. Because, indeed, a Marine—like America itself—is a tough fighter if necessary. But when allowed, each has a considerate, tender heart.

Whether it's gathering toys for needy children at Christmas, or airdropping food to the enemy in the midst of war, Americans much prefer a kinder, gentler role. Yet, they stand ever ready to do whatever is necessary to defend their way of life—their freedom.

At Babyland General that cold December night, I saw America at its finest. In the Marine serving his country. In the little girl showing respect. In everyday people giving their time and resources, wanting nothing more than for children everywhere to have a happy Christmas.

America—standing tall.
My America.
One nation, under God.

Published in Gainesville's *The Times* under title "Resolve mixed with tenderness" and on E-Zine: *2 the Heart. Reprinted with permission.*

Important note concerning copyrights: *Cabbage Patch Kids* and *Babyland General* are registered trademarks of Original Appalachian Artworks. *Toys for Tots* is a registered trademark of Marine Toys for Tots Foundation.

MEMORIES REVEAL TURNING POINT MOMENTS
Elouise Whitten

I shook my head
as if to clear my mind,
while I took one cautious step
after another
across the open plain
that I had tread before.

Again, I heard the explosions
that I once heard, erupting
behind me, around me,
and the memory of one corporal's body lifted high in the air,
plunging to the ground.
It was like hell on earth.

One private just behind me
yelled out, "Hey, Sarg,
I'm going to walk in your footprints,"
and he did.
We both made it all the way to the tree line
and safety.

As I held my son in my arms
I could almost hear him say
Daddy, I'm going to walk in your footsteps
and it gave me pause—it was a turning point-
to walk the straight and narrow line
in faith, on both occasions.

2006 *Northeast Georgia Writers*: First Place, Assigned Subject

A Penny Saved
Elizabeth Baumgardner

My first life-molding decision perhaps was when I was six years old—whatever my age, I was young enough to enjoy exploring a carnival with my father and old enough to realize it was more enjoyable, and possibly more lucrative, without my mother and older brother.

As we walked down the midway, I kept urging my father to win one of the prizes for me. He responded by explaining how the game was rigged or manipulated so that the customer won only at the Carney's discretion.

As we approached a penny toss game, my father dug down into his pocket for change, and said, "Here, you try your skill," as he fished out three pennies and handed them to me.

The Carney quickly interjected, "Hey, Mister, I'll give you pennies for all that change. I'll even give you pennies for a greenback!" When my father ignored his offer, he turned his attention to me, "All right, Girlie, step right up here and show what you can do!"

In the fenced-in area, most of the circles had single-digit numerals in them, but there were a few smaller circles with double digits or stars indicating a prize. The penny in my hand felt much lighter than the flat rocks I carefully chose for hopscotch, but as a pro I swung my arm a few times close to my side to line up a straight toss toward a star near the enter. My penny landed flat and nearly straight in front of me, but it was not near my selected target and seemed to be on the line around the circle.

"Excellent throw!" the Carney exclaimed as he quickly scooped up my penny. "That earns you three cents. Next time you're going to land on a star!" He handed me three brand new pennies.

Much to the Carney's surprise, to my father's surprise, even to my own surprise, I looked at the objects in my hand, frowned at the grid before me, closed my hand over my five cents, said "Thank you" to the Carney, and turned and walked away.

As with most turning points, this was not an instantaneous about-face. Family games always encouraged learning and thinking, stressing that more important than the "luck of the draw" or the "roll of the dice" was how it was used. My father's comments about the carnival games and my own inept toss emphasized the futility of this particular situation.

In retrospect, I have no idea whether "gambling" (and the suspense—or anxiety—involved) had lost its appeal or whether perhaps better possibilities (such as parental approval or a "sure thing" to brag about) had taken its place. I do realize that I now dislike taking chances and that, when I have to make a decision without enough facts, I try to consider the odds and make an educated guess.

2006 *Northeast Georgia Writers*: Third Place, Children's Fiction

WHAT CHRISTMAS MEANS TO ME
Samantha Brady

My Christmases have always been awe-inspiring. I remember when I was a young girl going to my grandparents' house every Christmas Eve and there would be a beautiful tree. It demanded attention no matter what the size or where it was in the room. I always stood there and looked at every Christmas Eve and there would be a beautiful tree. It demanded attention no matter what the size or where it was in the room. I always stood there and looked at every decoration on that tree and thought, how did she know where to put all these decorations? But that is not all that would inspire me.

Walking in I would smell cinnamon, my grandmother's favorite scent. She did not have to be cooking anything with cinnamon; just the smell would be in the room. I could also smell what she was cooking for dinner. When I was younger it was roast beef, but then later, it was usually turkey. Every meal was delicious, no matter what. I just knew when we were done; I would be full and satisfied.

Under the tree there were always a lot of presents. It looked like hundreds, but that was when I was a little girl. It still looks like a lot now, just some bigger than others. I was the only grandchild until my twenties so I got more presents than the others. Sometimes I still do.

My cousins live out of town and we don't get to see them or my uncle and his wife for Christmas so we just send them their presents and they send ours. It is too hard to go all the way to Florida just for a few days, although I would love to see them more often. I sure do miss my family.

I always love opening presents. It has always been my favorite time of the day. As I did then, I do now. I pass out the presents. Everyone calls me Santa Sam. I love this time, knowing that I give each person the pleasure of receiving the presents.

These days, I am even more inspired by what Christmas is all about. It is the most joyful time of the year for me as it should be for everyone. I know there are people out there who don't have good Christmases and I want to say to all of them – Go back to a time in your life when you were the happiest and remember it. Keep it in your thoughts all through this season. Don't let that thought go until you feel so happy or at least content you will not have a bad time. It will get you through this time and then just maybe you will have had such a good time you will start to love Christmas as much as I do.

Christmas has inspired me in so many ways that I have never had a bad Christmas even when something bad happened at that time – like when I was sick or hurt. I know I will be fine and have the most wonderful time. Let your Christmas be your inspiration to a much better life. It will help you with whatever you do.

As a writer, I have found that the thought of Christmas can help you through those really hard times when you are trying to come up with something to write. It gives me the kick in the pants I need to motivate my writing, no matter the topic. I think about putting a smile on someone's face when they read the words I put down on paper. I hope these words inspire you and bring you all the joy Christmas has to give into your heart. It does mine.

Merry Christmas and Happy New Year!!!
May all your dreams for the New Year come true.

A POET'S HEART
Blanche Buchanan Emerson

Poetry is for dreamers,
thoughts flow through our mind like streamers.

We hop, we skip, we jump and have fun,
but when the day ends we are never done.

We take out our pad,
and try to make other hearts glad.

It is through sharing our deepest thoughts about whom we are concerned,
that we've warmed the hearts of others to which we have turned.

So join me as we walk down the path of life,
throw away your sorrows and strife.

Put your trust into your Maker's Hands as he perfectly plans,
walk slowly and enjoy each flower for He watches our walk hour by hour.

He will help you conquer all the pitfalls that may come your way,
He will hold your hand every night and every day.

THE PEARL INSIDE
Julianna Ramsey

I'll never forget the day that it came.
It came sooner to others,
My pain was the same.

There was no forewarning
As I looked in the mirror,
Middle age glared out and shouted
I am here!

I'd thrown out the sheet music; I'd played my life free,
Setting my own tempo for what was to be.
But now I am impotent, so out of control,
My mirror tells me, darling, life has taken its toll.

I see wrinkles forming, and age spots appear
I see what is coming, and old age—I fear.
Once aging starts marching, there is no retreat,
A million good surgeons can't stop it for keeps.

The puzzle of a person that I'd come to be
Moved to the window, and stared out to the sea.
I pondered a pearl in an oyster, which over the years,
Becomes larger, more lustrous, while growing to be.
A pearl in the making, is my soul—it is me.

Like the shell of the oyster, my body is battered and worn
But the pearl of my soul is much larger, so I am not forlorn.
Its luster more glowing with more love than hate
A shell wide open to goodness, before it's too late.

The fog slowly lifted, sun came, I could see
Besides dreaded aging, sat things yet to be.
A life full of purpose, warm friendships anew,
And much more to savor, good works yet to do.

Escape from aging has but one door.
I am not ready to exit—
I want more, I want more.

Paradox
Diana Wildman

If individuality is so great a prize, then
Why do we struggle to be as the others?

If we could see through another's eyes
Would we be different or just like the others?

If color the same lest we despise
Would we be wrought to love one another?

If tongue be strange from fear we chastise
Would heritage be naught to us and the other?

If blood with blood doth mix we surmise
Would we be diminished by that of the other?

If neighbor from neighbor we oft' times devise
Would we abide noht uniqueness of other?

Our forefathers died for the freedom to be
Yet fearful of difference greatly are we!

THE TOWER OF BABEL
Harriet Woodcock

Oh, that we would speak in tongues
That others could understand,
Encircled in an arc of faith,
As we grasp a stranger's hand.

But, by speaking all at once,
We can only hear ourselves,
For crowds become extinct,
As inward they blindly delve.

Blaming it on a language gap,
This is what we hide behind.
For it eases our conscience bare,
And clarifies our cluttered minds.

If we listen with open hearts,
We can clear the thickening air,
And conceive every vocal phrase,
With utmost empathy and care.

Yet none of us translate well,
Due to prejudice and pride,
While struggling to confiscate
What we are feeling deep inside.

So like the Tower of Babel,
Where diversities are heard,
We fail to capture the meaning
Of the hastily spoken word.

For east is east, and west is west,
And never the peacemakers shall meet,
Unless they will strive to compromise
In the treacherous game of hide and seek.

As strong wills are oft-times obstacles,
When it comes to delicate mediation.
And good does not always seem to win out
If applied to self-seeking nations.

Now, we count our many failures,
In chances that have long gone by,
That we could form a peaceful world,
If all of us would only try.

And all should speak with one voice,
Praying out as loud as they can,
That their selfish ways will vanish,
As they embrace their fellow man.

©2003

LONGINGS OF A NONENTITY
Elizabeth Baumgardner

I do not exist. I am living matter that does not matter.
No one knows me as an individual. I do not exist.
Others may wish for fame and fortune; my wish is to be alive—
To be seen, to be heard, to be felt, to interact with others.

To be seen:
I am tired of being an uninteresting path to be bypassed
Or traveled as fast as possible. Should I try to slow the trip
By peering into someone's eyes, I am rebuffed by detached voids
As the person converses with himself or lectures down to me.
I am very tired of being made invisible by others.

To be heard:
I am frustrated that what I say is not thought worth listening to:
When someone answers conclusively—before I finish speaking;
When someone does not ask me to repeat, but does not understand,
as is obvious from his response, which may be irrelevant,
incomplete, redundant, or misleading—sometimes disastrously;
and especially, when my ideas are virtually ignored—
only to receive praise when expressed by an "important" person.

To be felt:
Literally, figuratively, I need an arm around me—
not a duty hug, a "hello," "good-bye," or "thank-you-for-the-gift,"
nor inebriated intimacy or erotic foreplay—
but a touch that says that I am a special individual
and that I am cared about because of, in spite of, what I am.

To interact with others:
I long to share the ramblings of my mind—reflective, complex thoughts
or fleeting whimsies—with any who will reply with repartee
or with exploratory probing, conversing as an equal—
not belittling my importance nor making me a sounding board.
I yearn for a spontaneous response not just a forced reply.

To be alive;
The fantasy world of my mind teems with plans, philosophies, dreams,
but without others' acknowledgement, my thoughts have no direction.
Before waves of despair carry me to the point of no return,
I need to become a vital participant in life's drama.

LOVE
Blanche Buchanan Emerson

V—Is for VICTORY over the grave. (success in defeating difficulties)

A—Is for ASSURED life after death. (guarantee)

L—Is for ultimate LOVE given freely from Jesus. (strong affection)

E—Is for ETERNITY. (infinite duration)

N—Is for a NEVER ending love for God. (not ever)

T—Is for TRULY believing in Jesus Christ. (genuine)

I—Is for an INEXHAUSTABLE love for God. (incapable of being used up)

N— Is for NONPAREIL life with God. (having no equal)

E—Is for the ELATED life we spend by knowing our Savior. (filled with Joy)

Places on the Journey

THE SUMMERTIME LAKE JAMBOREE
Lynda Holmes

Come on along with me
for a lazy day, picnic spree.
My cousins are here
and they greet me with cheer,
at our summertime lake jamboree!

The water is cold and so blue,
an azure-turquoise hue.
We are buoyant and light
with our life jackets on tight,
and I splash all around the view.

We alternate fishing and play,
tossing Frisbees around in the shade.
We race down the beach,
as sand covers our feet.
Then we drink down some cold lemonade.

When it's time for the evening meal,
My cousins and I say, "Good deal."
I smell grilled fish and steak
With potatoes just-baked
and I eat all the food with great zeal.

Now I'm full of food down to my core
as I stroll along the lake shore.
The sun blazes red,
making its bed.
Suddenly, I see it no more.

A loud boom resounds from on high,
as fireworks burst in the sky.
In unison we gaze
at the kaleidoscope haze:
Magenta-red, gold, and blue greet our eyes.

The fireworks and lake make a team
and create a wonderful dream:
The lake's all afire
in dazzling attire,
shimmering, yet still, in the moonbeams.

I'm glad that you came with me
for the lazy day picnic spree.
These memories won't fade
until new ones are made
at next summer's lake jamboree!

2006 *Northeast Georgia Writers*: Third Place, Poetry

VALENTINE'S DAY, NUMBER 65
Julianna Ramsey

It's Valentine's Day, my love, I say,
As we snuggle, cozy before the fire;
Warmly wrapped in the warm, fuzzy comfort of our peaceful souls,
This cold and icy day.

Together we share the out loud joy our squirrelly squirrels bring
As they munch and crunch and bounce and pounce
From tree to tree in the woods outside.

Throngs of hungry, chirping birds settle at our feeders,
Pushing and shoving, greedily picking out their favorite seeds;
Reminding us that we are each the chorus - for the other's solo.

Look, my love, a group of deer has come to forage in our woods.
Smug, they are, he says, knowing Taffy can't chase them away, as she barks
and growls at them from behind our hearth room window.

But my mind wonders, as we watch the linear pines and starkly nude oaks and
maples sway,
If we both will still be here to applaud their beautiful spring flowers
Or feel the orgasm of fall's annual triumph, when the trees stand proud in
blazing color
And then whirl and shake off their glorious robes to the ground,
Graciously giving the forest soft bedding for a long winter's nap.

Quit your wondering and enjoy the *now*, my love, he says,
And all the quiet pleasures between us and just outside our windows,
Given by God, free of charge, in a world where all else has a price.

Oh Valentine, most perfect Valentine, my gift today is you and I am yours.

YOU ARE NEVER TOO OLD FOR A HIKE IN THE MOUNTAINS OF BEAUTIFUL NORTH GEORGIA
Brenda Clark

Oh, for Pete's sake! I said to myself, *back away from the window! The last thing you want is for him to see you standing here anxiously peeping through the curtains as he pulls into the driveway. I might appear desperate and I'm not, really. I am just looking forward to seeing an old friend. It is hard to believe that we have known each other since the third grade. I wonder what he looks like? The last time I saw him was twenty years ago at our twenty-fifth high school reunion. We only talked a few minutes.*

Wait....here he is! Or, it could just be someone turning around in the driveway. No, I guess it is him. I hate dark car windows...I can't see his face.

Step back away from the window so that he will not see you while he is walking up the sidewalk. Oh, my heart is pounding! What is the matter with me? I am acting like a teenager. Calm down now, just calm down.

Hmmmm, not bad. A little less hair, but that is not a show-stopper. Mine is not as voluptuous as it used to be either. He really hasn't changed that much over the years. It looks like he has been taking good care of himself.

The doorbell...

Take your time answering the door. He does not need to know that you were standing behind it with your hand on the door knob. Let him ring the door bell and wait a few seconds. I doubt that he will turn around and run back to the car if you don't jerk open the door the minute he touches the door bell.

Fumbling with the two deadbolt locks and mustering every ounce of courage I could, I slowly opened the front door.

Awkwardly, I greeted him. He greeted me. We may have given each other a not-too-intimate hug. Quickly, I walked him around the house and into the kitchen, where I had prepared breakfast for us before we were to begin our day. There were biscuits, scrambled eggs with cheese, grits, sausage, fruit, orange juice and coffee.

"I hope you like everything that I have fixed," I said (before I discovered that he was a vegetarian and didn't eat white flour – so much for the biscuits, grits and sausage).

"This is perfect," he said, like a gentleman. He ate some of everything (the poor man must have been starved – before and after eating).

We chatted as we ate. No, actually, both of us picked at our food, and I *liked* everything on my plate. Maybe it was a case of nerves. After what seemed like hours, we cleaned off the table and he offered to help me clean up the kitchen while I put the dishes into the dishwasher.

We had planned to take a car ride up into the North Georgia Mountains where we would do a little hiking and eat lunch. He went to his car and started unloading all of the hiking gear he had brought. There were backpacks, ponchos (just in case it rained), a first aid kit, matches, a knife, a saw, bottles of water and a compass. No doubt this man was prepared.

"Okay," I said. "If that's everything, I will back my car out of the garage and we will load 'er up!" I volunteered to drive my car because he had been driving for a week from Louisiana to Florida to North Georgia and I thought he might like to have a break.

He stood by the little mound of hiking gear while I raised the garage door and cranked up my brand new, 5-speed, Mustang GT coupe. The vibration of that powerful 350HP engine shook the very ground that he was standing on. I slowly backed out of the garage and stopped in front of him. He had a rather stunned look on his face.

"How do you like my new car?" I asked.

He didn't answer.

"Do you think we can get everything into the trunk?" I asked. "What's left over can go into the back seat."

He still didn't say anything.

After much arranging and re-arranging, he got everything into the car and we were set to go. I had not been hiking in *years*. This was going to be fun!

He carefully maneuvered himself into the other half of the cockpit and hastily fastened his seat belt. (Maybe it was my imagination, but I was positive that I saw perspiration beads popping out on his upper lip). When we were both secure, I let the garage door down and turned on the ignition.

"Ready?" I asked.

Pause . . .

"Isn't this a muscle car?" he asked as he looked at me with a strange expression on his face.

"It sure is," I smiled. "I have wanted one of these sweet babies since I was a teenager. Want to see what she can do?"

Another pause . . .

"You'll love it, just wait and see," I said as I squealed off in a cloud of dust.

WITHIN THE SILENCE
Rosemary Harris-Mallinson

There is a quiet world where I can go,
Within the silence of my castle keep
Where sentient sounds which I have stored away
Evoke in vivid mental panoply,
Old cherished memories . . . of yesterday.

There I would roam in sweet abandonment
To listen to a canticle of spring,
The whispering wind through swaying hemlock trees,
A cardinal's whistled mating call at dusk,
And God's own voice that teaches me to sing.

Reprinted by permission from *In Search Of The Song,
Pathways To Communion*, © 2003

GOD'S BEAUTIFUL SUMMER SURPRISE
Julie Marlow

"Grandfather's farm is a nice place to spend summer vacation," Meghan declared, as the family drove into the tree-lined entrance. "We love coming to North Georgia." "Yes, look at the beautiful pond! I want to start exploring the pond right away!" said Ethan. "I know there are many fun things to do and watch there," said Sarah. They were all so excited; they all loved being on the farm. "Will we see big fish in the pond?" asked little brother Jack.

We are going to see many things and have lots of fun here," said Meghan, thrilled about the idea. The next morning was a bright and sunny day as Meghan, Ethan, Sarah and Jack started to the pond. Near the pond, they got into some tall grass and there, they came upon a huge nest. It was made of grass and weeds, and well hidden. Inside the nest were five eggs. "Oh, look at this bird nest!" exclaimed Meghan, as she looked closely. "What kind of birds do you think they are?" Ethan asked. "Meghan, will we see the little birds hatch out?" asked Sarah. "Well, maybe if we can stay here long enough," Meghan explained. Jack being the youngest of the four just wanted to pick up the eggs! "Humans are not supposed to touch the eggs," said Ethan, so Jack just walked off to see if he could see the fish in the pond.

Every day the children would run to the nest to look at the eggs and would wonder where the mother bird was. Maybe she is looking for food to give her baby birds when they hatch out, they thought. Anyway, that would be a good place for the mother bird to be.

Later, as the children were looking again to see the eggs, they suddenly heard Sarah shouting, "Look! The eggs are missing, they're all gone!" Jack hollered. Meghan, Ethan, Sarah, and Jack were very sad and Ethan asked, "Where did the eggs go?" Just as they were sitting there wondering what might have happened to them, Jack spotted something moving in the grass. There before their very eyes, five small birds were standing and what pretty, little birds they were! "I wonder what kind of birds they are?" asked Meghan, as she bent down to see them better. They seemed to be a little different from any bird she had seen before and as the children observed them carefully, they noticed that they had webbed feet. "They are ducks, they are ducks!" yelled Sarah. "Ducks will need to be in the water. They will be very happy to be in the pond soon," she yelled with excitement!"

For the rest of the summer, the children would run to the pond to see the ducks swim. Then one day, to their surprise, they saw a bigger duck swimming with the ducklings. She was tall and graceful, as she swam around the little ducks. "That must be the mother!" yelled Jack. Then, later that afternoon, they were excited to see the mother duck riding her family of five ducklings on her back. Oh, what fun it was to watch the duck family that day!

The ducks seemed a little clumsy at first, but now they were growing so fast that by the end of summer, their color began to change and they were beginning to look beautifully different. After the children had seen the mother, they began to wonder if the ducks would look like the mother as they got older. Curious, the children decided to check the encyclopedia to find out more about ducks. Yes! Right there on page 43, Meghan read all about ducks, geese and swans. They soon realized that the ducks they had watched all summer were not ducks at all. "They are swans!" the children yelled. The encyclopedia said that the swan is one of the largest birds and is closely related to geese and ducks, that the swan swims and flies gracefully, and its beauty has inspired composers, painters and writers. The children even found a "Danish Fairy Tale," a story about a Danish prince whose entire family was turned into swans. The only way that the family broke the spell was to fly off and fetch their sister, who was the only one that could help them to break the spell. What a fun story that was!

The children were so happy to find the birds that summer. Later, they watched the mother swan return to the pond to get her family and soon she was flying away making honking noises as her family joined her. Meghan, Ethan, Sarah and Jack were so happy to have witnessed such a great event.

The summer was gone now and the children had to return home; however, they all agreed this had been the greatest summer, each child saying that this would be a good memory for a long time. They hoped that when they returned next summer, the swans would come back too. They ran back and told their parents what a good summer this had been. Their parents said that some of the best memories come from summers like this and that good memories last forever. Then the parents explained a few things to the children. That all God's creatures have a message to show us; if we are observant and aware of God's creation; then we will know that everything God made is for our enjoyment. In addition, just like the swans they watched all summer, some people have a difficult time getting started in life; often, it is not until many years pass that they realize their great accomplishments. "All things are not always what they seem to be."[1]

Dear God,
Help us to see your great creation, and appreciate the wonderful world you have made for us. May we rejoice daily at your works. Amen

"Be thou exalted, O God, above the heavens; let thy glory be above all the Earth."
Psalm 57:5 (KJV)

[1] Quote by: Henry Wadsworth Longfellow, in The Poets.

OUR WOODLAND HOME
Leona Peffly Martin

We came to Georgia in 1982 and bought a house on a quiet cul-de-sac in the Stone Mountain area with woods behind it. I loved the tiny brook that trickled over the rocks on our property line. I loved to sit on the boulder just above it and watch the birds and squirrels, and the occasional deer rambling through the trees. We were contented there until the proliferation of shopping centers in the area, the four-laning of a nearby highway, and the building of a subdivision that wiped out my woodland view.

As we neared retirement, we dreamed of a home in the country. Grover wanted at least ten acres for a vegetable garden, fruit trees, berries and grapes. I just wanted a small creek. We couldn't stay in Gwinnett County where the cost of acreage was out of sight. We decided to go north up I-85, which would be more convenient for us while we were working. That search took up our weekends for a good while.

We tramped over many acres, but something was always lacking. Then we started working with an agent who had his own property for sale, and he thought we might be interested. We jounced down a long, twisting, and steep dirt road through the woods and stopped at the end. We could hear the sound of rushing water. As we moved down the trail, the music of the creek grew ever louder, reminding me of the creeks I had hiked beside in my native Washington state. We came to the top of a low bank. The creek was a good twenty-five feet across, and the water was churning over shoals, breaking around rocks, and creating eddies and swirls. The trees arching over the creek were green and lush. I sat down on a crude stone bench to drink in the view, but I was sure we could never afford such a gorgeous place.

We explored the area near the stream, we admired a spring that had been walled in with stone, and we realized how much work would be required to clear space for Grover's garden. We wondered if the open area where the owner had planned to build his house might be subject to flooding. We walked farther up the hill and found a perfect spot for our retirement home. Then we went back down to the creek, and I sat on the bench while Grover talked to the owner. His face was long as he came back. The asking price was nearly twice what we had decided we could afford.

We continued our weekend searches, but nothing suited us. After six months, we wondered if that property was still for sale. Might he come down on his price? When we called, he said yes, he still had the property, and he was willing to negotiate. He reduced his price a good bit, and we decided it was worth a large increase in our offer.

I still had some reservations. It was several miles from Homer with few neighbors nearby. Would we find friends? Could we manage as we grew older? We talked to our eldest son, who was living in a double-wide in a crowded trailer park near Buford. Would he be interested in relocating to our acreage? Yes, definitely!

We closed the deal and started spending weekends clearing space for Grover's gardens and choosing the ideal location for our house. Grover and our boys built an outhouse, a picnic ramada for our weekend lunches, and a shed for the tractor Grover had to have. He never could have cleared space for the gardens without it, and he uses it regularly to maintain our road.

Tim moved his mobile home and family to a spot at the top of the hill a couple of years before our house was built. We moved into our new house during a downpour. Both of our sons and our son-in-law were there to help, carrying the furniture into the house across a sea of mud. A couple of days after the move, I was surprised to hear the doorbell ring. When I opened the door, there stood Timmy and Katie. "We've come to visit you, Grandma," Katie said. What sweet neighbors!

At first we saw little wildlife. But we put up a bird-feeder by the kitchen window, and soon the chickadees, titmice, finches, sparrows and cardinals were in and out of it all day long. Then the squirrels came, too, and I've had a battle with them ever since! The deer finally got over their fear of us, and they are daily visitors now, which is a mixed blessing. I wanted a yard filled with beautiful shrubs and flowers, but the deer eat nearly everything I plant. They don't touch the daffodils—I think they are poison—and I have planted them everywhere. I found wild irises in the woods, but without blooms. I dug them up and put them in a sunny flower bed, and I have beautiful purple flowers every spring. I also found narcissus up the hill near the ruins of an old cabin and relocated some into my yard. So at least in the spring I have flowers.

But if I could choose between having a well-landscaped yard full of lush shrubs and colorful blossoms and having the graceful deer, I'd keep the deer. They wander by my kitchen window every morning and afternoon, sometimes pausing to look back at me as I enjoy watching them. I love our woodland home and wouldn't change a thing!

MY FATHER'S SPARE CHANGE
Brenda Clark

I was born a city girl,
Atlanta, Georgia is my native home,
I made a vow that I would never leave
And nothing would coax me to roam.

But, when I was young and the days were bright,
My father would often say,
"I have some spare change in my pocket,
So let's ride to the mountains today."

Then off we would go in the old family car,
I know we rode for hours
On roads that twisted and turned, climbed higher and higher
Through sunshine, shadows and beautiful wild flowers.

Just when I knew I would die of starvation,
A perfect picnic spot would appear
Complete with large shade trees and a babbling brook,
Where I waded without shoes or fear.

Mom would spread a homemade quilt on the soft, green grass
And hold the corners down with white stones,
Set out sandwiches, fried chicken, potato salad and pies,
When we finished, nothing was left but the bones.

I would rush back to play in the brook,
Wade up to my knees in water icy cold,
Sometimes, I would sit on a warm rock and watch the trout
Swimming upstream and shimmering like gold.

All too soon, the sun would begin to slide
Down behind the mountain ridges so high,
While Mom packed the food and Dad packed the car
I gathered my treasures, dried my feet and began to cry.

"Don't start that now," my mother would warn,
"You know it is time that we go,
But, if you'll be good and behave as you should,
We'll come back here before you know."

Alas, my parents have moved from their Earthly home,
I miss hearing my dear father say,
"I have some spare change in my pocket,
So let's ride to the mountains today."

Little did they know, so long, long, ago,
Of the love they instilled in my heart
For the beautiful North Georgia mountains,
Where I now dwell 'til death do us part.

WHAT DO THEY SAY?
Barbara H. Harper

To all who listen, they say, "WE ARE HERE."

To the poet, mountains speak a poetic language.

To the geologist, the archaeologist, and the biologist, they speak history – past and present – of earth and life.

If we are to hear mountains, we must listen with all our senses.

As travelers we stop to appreciate a distant misty-blue mountain range. It promises, "I belong to those who have eyes that appreciate." Memories cannot be bought, sold, or stolen from us. The mountains are ours!

Mountains declare presence. Their summits challenge some to climb. Others hear a challenge to cross through passes still hazardous or made easy by highways.

Summertime visitors yield to charms of literally audible rushing streams and waterfalls, and bird and animal sounds.

Poets hear the songs of the mountains and translate them into the written word.

To geologists, mountains speak through craters, upheavals, valleys, rocks, and soil. They "blab" their ages and origins; and tell tales of floods, droughts, eruptions, past climates, and earthquakes.

Archaeologists poke into secret pockets – buttoned tight by soil and years. The mountains grudgingly yield clues, or whole volumes, about man's intrusions on – and habitations in – these mountains.

Biologists touch, taste, smell, study and evaluate what the mountains "tell" them. The message may be, "Leave me alone!" Often, mountainsides willingly share natural products and medicines to better life and save it.

The mountains speak. Each person hears according to who he is.

1987 *Northeast Georgia Writers*: First Place, Assigned Subject

A Road Home
Barbara H. Harper

Something has ended. We cannot stay at the place we have been because the "place" is no longer there. We usually have choices as to which road to travel. If we do not like the roads offered, we can strike out through the wilderness and build our own road. I did just that after my husband died. In fact, I built that same road over and over. Winter rains washed it away. We walked in until repairs were made. The "wilderness" was a four-acre woods and the road was three-quarters of a mile long. That's not far to walk – unless one is carrying heavy groceries in heavy rain. We seemed moved off the planet when snow locked us in for seven days. Well, not that bad. The phone still worked – unless ice built up on lines.

Moving into our vacation cabin loosed me from accustomed moorings. I was lonely. A lucky accident provided a friend who introduced me to the natural world around me. She walked with me and put names to trees, and weeds magically became wild flowers. Insect pests became a learning challenge. The winter sky had stars. Had I never seen them before? The spectacular winter sunsets, the ever-changing lake water, tree shapes, shadows, a singing creek, and even rainstorms spoke messages I needed.

First the turning point, then the healing. Now that road I built leads to Home.

2006 *Northeast Georgia Writers*: Second Place, Assigned Subject

SOJOURN OF MY SOUL
Diana Wildman

My home is the refuge that comforts me
Tho' stone and mortar it may not be.
It echoes with whispers of souls that have been,
Of lives that were lost but may be again.

The path of my home, so near, yet far it wanders
From the spring where Cherokee tears
        Were quenched with cool waters.
Across the Red River to the vast prairie
To cathedral mountains standing in quiet reverie.

This path travels on to horizons far
Where a rock is home and lightning is caught
        In a clear Mason jar.
Where a young man dares to jump from planes
And a woman weeps when he goes to war.

This road well traveled takes me still
To highlands of heather where kilted clansmen dwell,
To emerald hills where haunting melodies my grief doth quell,
To a shimmering silver lagoon
        Where ancient spires mate with a brilliant black sky
        And a liquid lovers' moon.

As I travel to this secret place where only I abide
I hear the primitive jungle rhythms
        Where aboriginal bodies sway and glide.
I see the sweep of a Gaucho's hat as he bows and takes my hand
And leads me in a tango on the grassy Amazon lowland.

To this sanctuary, the path is now well worn.
It rests beneath a blanket of reds and golds,
For I am at my summer's end.
Yet I rejoice and do not mourn,
For I love this place of mine.
Ablaze with colors and passions fierce,
Tempered only by the river of time.

And when the snow comes,
Sweet and slow like a lover in the night,
I will hear the plaintiff wail of the beloved pipes
And the eternal fires in me will light.
Then my soul will depart this place
        To explore alone and unshackled in celestial flight.

2000 *Northeast Georgia Writers*: First Place, Unmetered Poetry

My Yard and Container Combo Experience
Elouise Whitten

In May 2003, I had a three-tiered deck built across the back of my house, with the expectations of garden beauty just beyond it. I had a gravel walk bordered with treated timbers installed that circled out half way into the back of the lot connecting one end of the decks to the other. I installed a decorative railed stair to the decks and added an arbor leading to the herb and vegetable gardens. I loved the project from the morning I woke up with the idea in my head and announced to my family, "I'm going to build a deck, a gravel walk and from now on we can enjoy a beautiful backyard, herb and vegetable gardens. Yes, I realized the beautiful backyard would require thought, money and work on my part. We had lived in the house for thirty-three years and I knew the steep yard slanting from left to right was easier to navigate when I was younger. I love the house, but one could do absolutely nothing in the yard except mow it. Even that was nearly impossible. The first time my husband tried it, he came in the house and put on his golf shoes for his safety to finish mowing the front yard. The next week I put the front bank back to nature, with five dogwood trees and azaleas and mulched the large, steep hill area with pine needles. I planted a five-foot magnolia tree between the dogwoods and the house. It now towers over 60 feet tall. I had added a flower garden and azaleas in beds on both sides of the driveway. That was all I'd done from 1970 until 2003.

After hearing my announcement, our married daughter commented, "Why after all these years are you doing this?"

Her question was reasonable. I answered with my reasonable answer, "Because I want to."

"No, really, why now, at your age?"

"Well, because I've been cooped up in the house long enough, I want to be outside on a flat surface. I fell in the yard three times last year and I want to see my vision of changes for our backyard."

This year, 2007, having learned the hard way, maintaining, digging and pulling weeds almost daily in several flower beds, herb and vegetable gardens, and having put over $500 worth of pine needles, around the azaleas, other shrubs, perennials and bulb beds, each year since, I had another "smart idea" how to decrease the cost and work for the beautiful additions this year. I am adding hanging baskets of cascading petunias and large containers.

My container gardening may not be a perfect science yet, but I have learned there are three basic ingredients—

<u>VERTICAL, FILLER AND TRAILING PLANTS</u>. When I mix those together in one container I virtually guarantee myself a perfect combination. When I shop for vertical additions to the container, I choose tall narrow plants, or I insert a small trellis for something that will climb in the center of the container. Some tall plants may need a stake for support or add some extra weight, such as rocks around the plant for ballast.

For VERTICAL PLANTS CHOOSE:
bronze fennel   red sage   spike (Dracaena) dwarf
papyrus   geranium
Oriental grasses   purple majesty millet

For TRAILING PLANTS CHOOSE:
dichondra   lamium
licorice vine   petunia
sweet potato vine   trailing begonia
lantana   ivy

For FILLER CHOOSE:
coleus   geranium
impatient   penta
verbena   begonia

    Add any of your favorite flowers to this mix and get started on building your own container additions to your front steps, patio, deck or garden. Be happy gardening this year. I am. I decided to give a gift to a friend by creating my first "year-around" planter with four perennials: a euonymus, with variegated yellow and green evergreen leaves, pruned to shape; an asparagus fern, and one large, sprawling, long-wide-leafed purple plant with dainty, pink flowers, and silver dusty miller. Then I added several colorful annuals of magenta impatient, pink periwinkle, white begonia and chartreuse sweet potato vines. When frost comes she will still have four different plant textures and colors that will look beautiful through the winter months. I plan to take her some pansies to brighten the container through the winter. When the pansies fade away, she can add colorful annuals of her choice next spring. Spread the joy.

2006 Northeast Georgia Writers: Third Place, Non-fiction Article

Death of a Village
Gloria Cassity Stargel

God is our refuge and strength, a very present help in trouble. Therefore will not we fear, though the earth be removed, and though the mountains be carried into the midst of the sea.
Psalm 46:1 (KJV)

It is an unsettling experience for a volcano to obliterate an entire village just when you're visiting that island. That's what happened during my first trip to Hawaii.

I long had dreamed of visiting our 50th State. So when my son Randy invited me to go I said "Yes!"

Soon after arrival on the Big Island, I learned one doesn't just *visit* Hawaii. One *becomes* Hawaii. The spirit of the Islands proves contagious. The wonderfully pleasant trade winds, the incredibly beautiful iridescent ocean, the warm hospitality of the people, the glimpses of an ancient culture—all transport you into a different world.

In our vacation condo by the sea, I quickly unpacked, donned my new flowered muumuu that reached to the sand, and draped a lei of plumeria blossoms around my neck. I was ready to *become* Hawaii.

So it was that when Randy returned from a walk, I heard his news with some concern: "Did I tell you one of the volcanoes here is still active?"

"No," I said, holding in mid-air the pitcher of pineapple juice I had been pouring, "I don't recall that you did." There in our tropical paradise, it was difficult to imagine that just thirty miles away a volcano was spewing molten lava.

Surrounded by black lava fields, though, one recalls how these islands were formed. How over millions of years, volcanic eruptions that began on the ocean floor kept building up hard surfaces until they finally appeared above water. The result is this intriguing land of contrasts—volcanic deserts and ocean-swept coastlines, rolling pasturelands, lush tropical valleys and snow-capped mountains. All within Hawaii's 93 x 76 miles.

Ever since January 3, 1983 with Kilauea Crater's spectacular "fountaining"—that explosion from deep within the earth, which shoots fire a thousand feet into the air—the liquid rock had continued to ooze out of the vent in a hot, gray mass. Looking like something from a horror movie, it spread out, going its own way toward the sea. At 2,000 degrees, it consumed everything in its path.

All the while, residents of Kalapana had watched the progress of its coming toward them, hoping the creeping mass—somehow—would be diverted. However, that week in early May of 1990, the lava flow accelerated from the Puu O'o vent of Kilauea. The volcano became front-page headlines and television newscasts aimed their cameras toward the village of Kalapana.

It had been an agonizingly slow death for Kalapana. Now the end came quickly as the lava flowed faster—and faster. What had been an orderly evacuation gave way to panic as residents grabbed whatever they could and fled, just minutes before the hot lava covered the village's only remaining road, leaving Kalapana encircled by the relentless flow that devoured 142 dwellings.

"If only there were something we could do to help," I said. "Yet the last thing they need right now is a lot of tourists getting in the way." *There is something I can do, though*, I told myself. *I can pray for those people undergoing such trauma. I can pray they will know God's peace in the midst of the storm.*

"Have you seen this?" Randy asked the next day, handing me a newspaper. It showed a little church building, loaded on a trailer, being moved away from the path of destruction. It barely made it out in time.

As for the displaced persons of Kalapana, many were living in tents set up at the nearby park along the beach. Soon, this area, too, was being invaded by the fiery fingers of lava — smoke, steam and acid fumes creating a health hazard Even more so when the lava struck salt water, causing much roaring, hissing, and crackling, and producing hydrochloric acid and other potentially hazardous emissions in the blast of steam.

I grieved for the people of Kalapana. Some of them had lived there for generations. They gathered in the park now to say good-bye to their homes, their dreams, their way of life. They sought out old friends, embracing warmly, smiling — more than a few of them smiling through tears.

In the midst of their own grief, though, the people knew that here is where creation and destruction meet. They knew that, even now, the volcano was breathing new life and adding new land for generations yet to come.

Witnessing this phenomenon made me ponder the awesome power of this One, of whom it is said in His Word: *May the glory of the Lord endure forever; may the Lord rejoice in His works, who looks on this earth and it quakes and trembles; who touches the mountains and they smoke!* (Psalm 104:31, 32; AMP.)

Most native Hawaiians are Christians and not far away—by the side of the road—as a silent symbol of devotion to the Lord God, the little church atop its trailer swayed in the wind.

I returned home to the mainland with a prayer for the people of Kalapana. I prayed they would gain strength and hope from the rescue of that brave little church. And that wherever the church put down new roots, the people, too, could replant and rebuild. Rebuild a community of faith. Faith in this One, our Most High God, Sovereign of the Universe.

Published in Gainesville's *The Times* in my three-part series:
"*Aloha means hello – and goodbye.*"

A Magical Hour
Kate McConnon

The weather was perfection. Crisp blue sky with a balmy wind that gently brushed your hair and made the warm sun seem the perfect intensity. San Jose, Cost Rica on a leisurely Saturday afternoon. My husband, Pat and I were strolling down an arcade as wide as a street with shops on either side. Shops which for us held no interest, filled with electrical appliances, children's toys, and discounted post holiday items. Somehow Christmas decorations always look bedraggled after the fact but today the weather and the sky and the easy-going crowd made even the week-old displays seem festive and right.

We ambled up to a small plaza between a large impressive bank and a museum with a huge sculpture displayed on a concrete block of taut, muscular farm laborers straining at their work. Lacy fig trees, huge compared to the houseplants we have in our homes and offices in North America made sun-speckled shadows on a gurgling fountain and the people sitting and standing under their boughs.

All eyes were turned toward a group of Andean musicians easily recognizable by their high cheekbones and lush black hair bound up in a ponytail or under a hat. Their music was utterly captivating, the pulsating drum and the reverberating flute in perfect synch with the throbbing guitar strumming. The effect was as powerful as a tuning fork the way that it echoed throughout your body.

And we were all mesmerized---we tourists from Georgia, old wrinkled women out for a lunch, young lovers strolling arms intertwined, families with wonder-eyed children taking in each beat and stroke. There were smokers out for a break, leather-dressed teens out strutting. All of us paused and drank in the elixir of the music and the day. It wasn't a tapping, hand clapping crowd although the music reverberated within each one of us; it was a moment of total attention and pleasure shared with strangers.

An elderly, short, wiry man, his face creased and weathered with one front tooth and a jaunty little red hat came upon us. He had a small crinkled brown paper bag clutched in his hand and as his eyes riveted on the musicians his feet moved in an irrepressible dainty step that you knew he had done before, probably in his native country. It was obvious that he was one of them—a musician. At some time in his life he had played, he had danced, he had made this very music and this Saturday afternoon as he was probably on some routine errand he was reliving that celebration of the flutes and drums under the sun-dappled figs with the rest of us. It only made it richer to watch his joy and contentment as we all felt the music. It was a magical hour that we spent in that plaza, a magical show we all shared in, better than any planned "show" could ever be.

Standing Strong
Samantha Brady

Poem for America
September 11, 2001

The World Trade Center stood proud and strong for 30 years,
But now it is in ruins.
Because terrorists destroyed it with planes.
All those people gone is so tragic and sad.
But America will go on and stand tall.
We will not stand for this terrorism.
For we are brave and proud.
We are the heroes of yesterday, today and tomorrow.
We are Americans.
We will unite.
The terrorists will be caught for America is strong.
God Bless America, the Home of the Brave.

People on the Journey

THE IMPACT OF A FICTIONAL MARIA
Laura Leigh Harris

Can a free spirit, one filled with individuality and life, influence another? Can a woman, seen as difficult by some and darling by others, win over her skeptics? Though *The Sound of Music* features a woman who leaves the abbey to become a wife and mother, is it possible for this semi-fictional Maria von Trapp to change a little girl's outlook on life? The answer is "Yes." To this day, my heart is moved every time I watch this musical because of Maria's practicality, love for others, and humility.

While Maria longed for adventure, she sometimes feared the unknown. And, though she possessed a natural tendency to run when faced with adversity, she eventually learned to stand firm and face her problems. She respected the authority position over her, whether the Captain or the Mother Abbess, yet remained secure in her independent thinking. Strong initiative helped her to unravel the knots of life and discern the reasons for her trials. Given the fact that her confidence and talents drew envy from those less secure in their identities, she continued to move forward. The coupling of her industrious skills with her creative and musical talents produced lucrative family synergy.

When standing face-to-face with life's challenges, she relied on her faith in God as her source. Her faith encouraged her to look for open windows when the doors slammed shut. She learned to appreciate the storms of life and taught others not to be afraid. Instead, she encouraged others to focus on their favorite things. She made the best of life, no matter the circumstances, and led others to new heights.

Once she dealt with the ever-present guilt of not serving God as a nun, her confidence grew with the realization that she did God's will by obediently returning to the children (and the man) whom she loved dearly. Not only did she become the glue that held the von Trapp family together, but also God blessed her and her family with the ability to bring musical entertainment to thousands. To this day, her grandchildren still bless others with their gifted voices.

Maria's example continues to provide a detailed road map of direction for my life. When I am frustrated or discouraged, I revisit the role model she provides for a full and vivacious life. She reminds me not to close people out, but instead draw them closer. She reiterates the need to stand firm when faced with adversity, instead of running to the hills. Choosing to rely on my faith in God and His strength, I don't sweat the various kinks of life.

Maria allowed God to help her climb every mountain, ford every stream, and follow every rainbow. And because of that, she found her dream. I can too!

2007 *Northeast Georgia Writers*: Second Place, Assigned Subject

COUSIN LUTHER
Norval P. Caples

Cousin Luther knew nothing of Asiatic or Arabic languages. In reality, he knew only English, but he was quick and caught on fast. In 1936, at 19, he'd gotten hired to pick snap beans for a commercial cannery. This put him in contact with many Polish speaking families from the big city that were earning considerable monies during the depression years, with whole families engaged in nimbly picking snap beans for about a penny a pound and having temporary living space and transportation to and from the fields thrown in.

The foreign-born parents all spoke Polish, many of them no English at all, but the children, educated in U.S. schools, were equally fluent in both languages. When he went out in the bean fields, Luther found himself surrounded by workers, all speaking a foreign language.

This posed no problem for Luther. Just about as naturally born book-smart as they came in those days, Luther could hear or read something one time and he had it down cold, and if he'd missed anything, his abilities could quickly fill in the gaps. Not yet wise enough in the ways of the world or confident enough in himself to let those pretty girls with the flashing eyes and red kerchiefs find him, Luther set out to learn Polish and impress them in that way.

It took quite a few days of diligent observation and listening, but Luther was getting the hang of it. Foreign languages weren't exactly new in Carroll County. Most of our parents, whose ancestors were originally from the British Isles, could speak some German. From the 1870's onward, there had been an influx of German immigrants escaping conscription for service in the Franco-Prussian wars and many settled in Carroll County where they quickly became leading citizens as they prospered in this new land. As time went on, less and less German was used and our generation learned only fragments of the language.

Despite his background (7th grade) and limited preparation, Luther soon felt confident enough to announce to the bi-lingual teenagers surrounding him that while he might not be able to pronounce the words, he could understand every language except Greek. They bit. First, they tried their own language on him. He held up his hand, "Slow down, don't hold me to complicated stuff even you would have trouble with." Luther then did pretty well, and they were impressed. Luther nudged things along, "Try German." He easily handled the few words that they were familiar with. Those Poles weren't dumb; among them they began coming up with all sorts of words and sounds unrelated to any language Luther had ever heard.

Luther would appear to go into a deep study and slowly shake his head as first one and then another would supply a word or a phrase in a language that would stump him, but even then Luther was prepared. Looking deliberately around, he'd announce, "Those unfamiliar words and phrases--they all sound like Greek to me."

2007 *Northeast Georgia Writers*: Award Winner

WHAT IS A MENTOR?
Samantha Brady

A mentor is a Teacher as well as a friend.
A mentor will help you through the thick as well as the thin.
A mentor will lend you a helping hand.
Throughout the good and the bad, the happy and the sad.
A mentor will help you through it all.
A mentor will give you advice and teach you all about your goal.
All throughout your life.
That is what a mentor means to me.
Thank you for being my mentor as well as my friend.

For Elouise Whitten

MY FIRST VALENTINE
Julie Marlow

Oh! What a Valentine's Day
When Cupid's arrow came my way.
Stunned, I glanced, then a grin,
The card I clutched, I knew he made,
Three little words my classmate wrote,
"I Love You"
Those innocent words were but a few,
They were the only words he drew,
On the red paper heart,
but as for me, a special joy,
My first Valentine card
from the little boy
on the next row.

YUHLON
Norval P. Caples

The year 1937 saw the Depression ease off a little for small landowners in Carroll County, Maryland. It would set in again the next year, grinding hard-working farmers further down, but they didn't know that then.

Arthur H. Griffee, Winfield Elementary School's far-sighted principal, saw an opportunity to promote health and well-being within the student body while maintaining the school's always high academic standard. Mr. Griffee, with the zeal of a reformer, stressed good grooming and personal hygiene and decreed that slovenliness would not be tolerated. Henry quickly saw that school, especially the sixth grade, was going to be different that year. This would be the third consecutive year to have Miss Franklin for his teacher, but that wasn't a problem. Sixty years afterward Henry still tells everyone who will listen, that half of this entire education was crammed into those years as Miss Franklin's pupil.

During the fourth and fifth grades, there had always been the next higher level of students on the other side of the classroom. Henry found himself, as a sixth grader, in an unfamiliar setting. When the teacher would instruct the fifth graders, there was now nothing new to be learned by listening in, and he quickly became bored and restless. Miss Franklin had prepared for all that; Henry was assigned a front seat alongside the wall, and Yuhlon, absolutely the best behaved girl in the room, occupied the desk behind him.

With little to do except daydream, fidget, and read the books Miss Franklin somehow spirited to him from the normally locked-up library, Henry was facing a long school year going over the same sixth subject matter he'd listened in on throughout the year before.

Yuhlon, cool and possessing the calm self-assurance that pretty girls seem to be born with, surprised Henry by becoming friendly almost at once. Miss Franklin, whose aim had been to isolate the disruptive lad as much as possible, seemed equally surprised to note how well this unlikely pair got along.

Except for frequently telling Henry to turn around and do his work, Miss Franklin didn't seem to mind him and Yuhlon whispering together all that much. After all, Yuhlon, in her own way, served as a super substitute teacher who steered the rambunctious Henry toward acceptable classroom behavior, easily and naturally.

True friendships require some give and take on both sides in order to flourish, Henry had read somewhere, so he tried to listen carefully and speak on subjects of interest to Yuhlon. She could sew well; so could Henry. He really could, but Yuhlon could do so much more; she could skillfully make many of the clothes she wore. She could probably cook and bake, too, but Henry didn't ask.

Yuhlon, innately sensitive, dignified, and proper, and Henry, her opposite in practically every way, went through the entire school year without a fight or cross word. Yuhlon would simply clam up and turn away if Henry began to be dominating or argumentative, and Henry quickly realized that social isolation was really no fun at all. Their togetherness was confined to the classroom. Yuhlon had her own circle of friends during lunch period and recess times, and they saw little of each other during "playground time."

Miss Franklin had placed a sealed box decorated with red hearts on her desk a week before Valentine's Days, and students began to drop valentines through the narrow slot at the top. Valentine's Day was an event, and excitement ran high as the gaily-decorated cards were passed out. Yuhlon sent Henry a Valentine that year. Deep down, he suspected she'd sent a valentine to other boys as well. But he put aside that thought at once. It was a modest valentine, no ruffled lacework or moving parts, but to Henry it was the grandest of all. It pictured two Swiss kids, a boy and a girl in native costume playing in a mountain meadow. The message was, "ALPINE FOR YOU, Be My Valentine," signed Yuhlon.

The next year, Yuhlon did not occupy the desk behind Henry and the bond between them, a fragile classroom thing, was broken. Later on, Henry dropped out of high school, and Yuhlon quit school and got married when she was seventeen.

Yuhlon's father, Donald, had been hired to bring his tractor and equipment to saw stove wood for Henry's Uncle Jack, and Henry was helping. Donald brought along a young man and introduced him as Yuhlon's husband. Henry's heart sank. They worked side by side for several hours and despite all the noise and the tension that Henry felt, the two young men communicated and worked well together. Somehow, Henry could better handle the fact that Yuhlon's husband was a stranger and not someone he and Yuhlon had gone to school with.

Donald invited Henry and his uncle to a reception for the newlyweds that was to be held that very night and added, speaking in Henry's direction, "Bring everybody." Henry relayed the message when he got home and surprisingly, his father agreed to go.

They got ready and began walking the mile and a half in time to arrive as darkness was beginning to fall. Uncle Jack's house was on the way, and they found him waiting to see who would be showing up to join him. The three of them then walked the remaining distance together.

Henry was pleased to have been invited, but as they neared the house, ablaze with lights, where many guests were already gathering amid shrieks of greeting and laughter, he began to get cold feet. Well, he was glad he didn't come alone; his father and uncle would know how to act and fit in among so many strangers. Just as they reached the driveway, they were met by Yuhlon's father, driving hurriedly away amid a clashing of gears. He saw the three of them, slowed down, yelled a cordial greeting, and added, "I'll be back in just a little while; you folks go on in."

Henry was surprised to note that his two mature companions didn't seem to know what to do next and acted as if they felt as ill at ease as he did. They sat down on the frosty lawn grass feeling conspicuous and out of place, dressed so ordinarily and too self-conscious to join a glittering assembly of strangers. Without a word of discussion, the three arose in unison and headed homeward. Henry stood in the dark shadows, pausing a moment to look again at the house, all aglow and vibrating with gaiety. Silhouetted in a window stood Yuhlon, radiant—glancing for an instant toward Henry—but not seeing him in the darkness.

APRIL PARADOX
Marsha Hopkins

Death and taxes – those are the certain things. (I had known this since second grade when someone asked our teacher if we HAD to write our names on our papers – "All you HAVE to do is pay taxes and die!" she had announced to a room full of startled seven-year-olds.)

Anyway, those two arrived together this year – unwelcome, dreaded, but not unexpected. They followed the most beautiful springtime in many years and they slipped in the door just after Easter's silent exit.

How can a single month hold such piercing beauty and such numbing sadness?

My friend, you were so brave in knowing it was time for you to go – that it was time to leave all that had harnessed you in a life less vibrant than you had always known. Your favorite redbuds held their tiny blossoms far longer than usual this year, but on Easter, they finally gave way to fresh, lime-rich leaves as they dropped to cover the ground in lavender.

I will miss your contagious laughter, your keen wit, and your warm spirit. I will replay the good times over and over in my heart. I will do what I HAVE to do, but I will also make the most of the rest of my life.

I learned so much from April – and from you.

2006 *Northeast Georgia Writers*: Award in Poetry

THE BIRDER
Patsy C. Paget

I gave my love a Bird Field Guide to help identify
The myriad of bird species that daily caught his eye.

He bought his first binoculars, and then a telescope;
He planned that he'd go birding every day when he awoke.

For years with expectation he began each brand new day
Anticipating all the birds that just might come his way.

He listened to the songs birds sang and memorized their calls.
He studied their behavior in the Winter, Spring, and Fall.

He kept a daily record of the birds that he had seen.
He started reading articles in birding magazines.

He joined a local birding club; subscribed to Audubon.
He learned of expeditions that he'd like to go upon.

His friends were all called Birders and their passion was the same.
He met them on the weekends and they played their birding games.

They talked of rare bird sightings and they gave each other tips;
Kept day lists, state lists, life lists; and they went on many trips.

He's upgraded his binoculars and now can see so far
With help from his new telescope, one crafted by Questar.

His shelves of foreign field guides and his walls of birding notes
Bring memories of Birding tours in places quite remote.

Oh, had I know the impact of this gift of long ago;
How his obsession with the sport would grow and grow and grow;

Would I have bought a Bird Cookbook? This thought has oft occurred;
But mostly when he's far away----Communing with the birds.

> 1996 *Northeast Georgia Writers*: Second Place, Poetry
> Published in "GOSHAWK," September 1996
> (Newsletter of the Georgia Ornithological Society)

ADVENTURE VS. WEDDING BELLS
Margaret Stout Ellett

A group of us were in the nurse's barracks talking about the wonderful adventure ahead of us. There were 300 of us getting ready to go overseas. The war was finally over and we were being sent to replace nurses in the European Theater. I was called to the phone. It was the C.O. asking me to come to his office. I quickly gathered up some papers I thought he wanted and headed for his office. He was standing outside talking to a nurse, but told me to go on into his office. I walked in and who did I discover but my boyfriend, Bob. He had driven to Columbia, SC from Camp Campbell, KY. He hugged me saying, "I came down to marry you if you will have me and if you can get out of the army." I had no hesitancy. I would gladly give up this overseas adventure to marry this man. We talked to the C.O. Since the war was over, nurses could get out of the army who had served 3 years or were over 35 or were married. The problem was he could not give me a leave since I had overseas orders. He said just get lost - which actually meant I went AWOL.

Since Bob did not know the laws in South Carolina, he decided we should drive over to Augusta. Georgia. On the way, we stopped for lunch. While waiting for our food, Bob said, "Let me show you something." He pulled out his wallet and handed me his driver's license. Looking at this, I said, "This says your name is Shelly Randolph Ellett." He said that is right. Then explained that his friend thought his middle initial, R was for Robert, and had started calling him Bob. He hadn't bothered to correct him - so eight months ago the friend introduced him to me as Bob. All the time we dated, I called him Bob and he called me sugar.

After lunch, we drove on to Augusta and directly to the courthouse. We found we had to have two witnesses to get our marriage license. We went out on the steps but everyone came along one at a time. Then Bob - err Shelly said, "Come on." We jumped into his Dad's old Plymouth and Shelly drove to the bus station. He ran in and came out with a young couple. They went to the courthouse with us, signed our marriage license and then we took them back to the bus station.

We were married in the study of the First Baptist Church in Augusta. Afterwards, I called my mother. I had promised I would call her just before leaving the states. Hearing my voice, she started to cry. "Are you leaving? Do you know where you are going?" I said, "No, I'm not leaving. I got married!" Starting to cry even harder, Mother said, "You got married!!! To Bob?" she asked. She had never met this man but I had told her about him. I said, "Well no. His name is Shelly; but it is the same man. Mother said, "I don't understand" I said, "It's O.K. Mom. You'll meet him soon and you'll love him too."

A Special Day Just for Dad
Margaret Stout Ellett

It wasn't until after I joined the Army Nurses Corps during World War II that I discovered how much my joining the army really meant to my dad. It seems when he was with a group of men; they were always talking about their sons in the services. It made Dad feel very unpatriotic, since he had no one to brag about. Now he did.

Dad was never one to give direct compliments; but through the years, we often found out that he had bragged about his three girls to his friends and acquaintances. I well remember a special day in his life when I was directly involved in his bragging.

Home on a three day pass, I was enjoying relaxing and visiting with my parents, catching up on family and local news. Dad asked me if I would put on my uniform and go to town with him. Wanting to please him, I went upstairs and changed into my uniform, taking extra care to look neat and trim. Joining my parents, I thought I looked pretty good, but together, Dad and I retied my tie three times.

We drove the mile and a half to the small country town of Sulphur Springs, Indiana located at the intersection of State Road 36 and Henry County Road 300 West. A little apprehensive about what Dad had in mind, I got out of the car and walked with him to the grocery store. There, we had a soft drink and chatted with owner Keith Fadley, his son, and a few customers.

From there, we walked across the street to the bank. I was beginning to relax a bit as we talked to our long time friends there. But then Dad surprised me by heading for the barber shop. Thank goodness, I found a few men I knew among those waiting for haircuts.

We came out of the barber shop and turned left. "Dad, not the pool hall. I've never been in there!" Dad just grinned. In the front door we went. Fortunately, we didn't tarry. Just in the front door and out the back as the men stared.

Dad was heading for the car and I breathed a sigh of relief; but then Dad drove down the street to the garage to have the brakes checked. Of course, they were okay. Then, after a stop for an ice cream cone, we were finally on our way home.

As I looked over at my dad, I saw this special look of pride and joy as he nibbled away on his ice cream cone. My frustration over the experience gave way to affection and amusement.

Several years after my dad's death in 1967, I was visiting my mother. As we talked in the living room, she looked up at a photograph of me in my army uniform. Taken many years ago, it still hung in a very prominent place. "Your daddy loved that picture." She said. "He never wanted it taken down."

Thanks Dad for your patriotism, for your pride in your family and for your love.

Daddy's Cubbyhole
Margaret Stout Ellett

Down in the basement behind the furnace, was Daddy's Cubbyhole. It was always there. Well, at least from the time we moved to the farm in 1928, when I was a little girl.

It was located in the area of the basement having a raised wooden floor, built over the cement foundation; it was heated and had a small high window. Thus, it was quite comfortable in spite of appearance. The outside cement block wall was lined with bookshelves. Additional shelves, an old cupboard, and a filing cabinet were placed against the interior sheetrock walls. His desk was at right angle to the outside wall, allowing him to face the entrance to the tiny nook. In winter, to keep the heat from escaping into the rest of the basement, an old piece of canvas hung over the doorway opening into the larger room.

In spite of an artistic eye and a civil engineer degree, neither walls nor shelves lined up to give straight lines and square corners. Dad had pretty much thrown the room together with odds and ends of leftover scraps of wood. These were the depression years and most of us just made do.

Everything was always thick in dust. You might say Dad often blended right in, as he relaxed at his desk for an hour or so after lunch, before returning to the field. Mother had no desire to add this cluttered space to her cleaning chores, and Dad was happy to have his various 'project piles' left undisturbed. These often extended out into the larger room, which was also ignored by Mother.

Daddy had more time to spend in his little corner during the winter months and when it rained. Year around, most evenings found him there for a few hours. However, after supper, especially on winter evenings, he always found time to play checkers, carom, or another board game with us three girls before heading for one of his projects. In those days, there was no T.V. and our radio was only turned on for special programs such as "Amos and Andy," "Will Rogers," "The Music Hour," "News," and the "Market Reports." Sometimes Daddy would be in his cubbyhole just before or just after supper. Often, while helping Mother in the kitchen, we girls would discuss different subjects with her—from school and everyday problems to sibling disagreements to philosophy of life. Intent on our conversation, we would forget that Dad might be listening. You see, the kitchen register and duct leading to the furnace was almost above his desk, giving him an 'earshot' ringside seat. He usually would remain quiet; but occasionally, if his strict, old fashion ways did not approve of the direction the discussion was taking, he would give himself away, by yelling up to us, stating his opinion. One evening, after spending the afternoon at the county fair, I was so excited. "Mother, I met this cute boy at the fair. He got a better score than I did in showing off our pigs. We had so much fun. I think he might ask me for a date." Mother asked me a few questions about where he lived. Dad voice came from the basement, "No way you can go out with that boy until we find out who he is and who his parents are." Being cute, in 4-H club, and showing a prize pig just wasn't sufficient information.

Dad did have his projects; many, many of them - from business to community concerns to personal crusades, to interests and hobbies.

In late winter, I enjoyed watching him make his dolls - corn dolls to test percentage of germination of various varieties of corn from various fields. Cutting long strips of newspaper; he would lay the strips lengthwise and then place corn kernels that he labeled along the strips as he rolled the papers up into a fairly firm roll. He would keep these rolled corn dolls moist and in a warm place. After a time, at various intervals, he would unroll the dolls to check for the degree of germination.

A few years after moving to the farm, Dad worked with Purdue in developing Hybrid Corn. He then raised and sold Hybrid Seed Corn. I would help by detasseling three rows and leaving one, for what seemed many, many weeks, as the corn grew to maturity.

Daddy was very community conscious. Prepared by study and research, he gave many talks in our county and adjoining counties, supporting Manual Training and Career Guidance in High School. For years, he campaigned for consolidated schools rather then one in each township. He supported his speeches with various charts of figures and graphs. As I think back, I marvel at those neat detailed charts produced in that cluttered and dirty basement.

Dad also was a member of the first County Planning Board. He had an office in town with the board, but spent much time doing research in his own cubbyhole.

Another favorite subject of his was the history and statistics on farmers migrating west and what the future held for farming. He also enjoyed genealogy research, photography and sketching. Later years found him planning trips, which he and mother enjoyed.

Years after his death, while staying with mother a few weeks, she kept trying to talk me into going down to the Cubbyhole to start clearing it out. I finally went down but could do very little. I felt so like I was trespassing. I slowly started checking files and did enough to realize how rough it was those first years living on the farm. It was shocking to review financial records and later tax records, which showed how very meager the farm income had been during those early years. In addition to it being the Depression Era, Grandpa had left a large debt in the form of a mortgage on the farm. Somehow, our parents managed and maintained a happy home and we girls never realized how poor we really were. After all, our friends and neighbors were in the same boat.

Daddy had quite a library of books covering many, many subjects. Surveying the shelves, I carefully selected books for Mother to inscribe and give to her 12 grandchildren and to their parents. They will appreciate these books from Dad's library, I thought, as I carefully dusted the stack. Down on one shelf: I spotted a couple of "sex books." I laughingly pointed them out to mother. Her initial look of surprise quickly turned to one of concern, worried for fear a visiting farmer might have spotted them and been critical of Dad.

While seldom verbal in his praise, filed clippings and snapshots here and there, attested to his pride in his family.

Checking out his files and detailed records, I mused at how much I was like him. He filed all sorts of clippings, probably never again to be read - but then maybe. That is I too. And also, all those records!! Included were detailed records on Hybrid Seed Corn and on farm expenses and profit.

Like him, I am always working on many projects, which create much clutter. I will say I do a better job dusting.

Finding his files of statistics, notes, chapter outlines, and completed chapters, I was saddened that he never finished the book he was writing on the migration and the history of farmers and farming in the Midwest. Then again, I know the pleasure he had in gathering together the bits of information and satisfying his own quest for knowledge.

Closing the file drawer, I looked about the room. Amid the familiar clutter and dust, I spotted a fond reminder of Dad. On the bookcase by the desk was his green visor, to protect his sensitive eyes. The visor left behind, he had made his own migration to another place.

Samuel Ernest Stout, 1885–1967

A DOSE OF HUMOR
Harriet Woodcock

My father, John, was an inspiration to all who had the privilege of knowing him. He was a pharmacist, and he loved filling prescriptions. But he was still from the old fashioned school of thought that believed "laughter was the best medicine."

His customers cherished his sense of humor. Even the elderly country women loved his greetings. Clutching their handkerchiefs filled with change, they would painstakingly search for the right coins. As John neared the prescription window, he would call out, like the barker in the circus, "Have your money ready." For those customers who called in to have their merchandise delivered, there was the lady who ordered a hot dog. "Do you want to have the wiener all the way?" John asked patiently. The customer came back haughtily, "What did you want me to do? Meet you at the Methodist church?"

On other occasions, patrons would call and say, "Give me the fount." And my father would reply, "Sure, come and get it. You're more than welcome to it." John wanted to make all of his customers feel right at home in his Rexall Drug Store. So he added a soda fountain, ice cream tables and chairs, and make-up booths. There was everything from cosmetics to candy, to cigars. So when John wasn't filling prescriptions, he was right there entertaining his clients.

"Here is a pen that writes red, yellow, and green," John would say confidently as he handed the onlooker the writing instrument. Grabbing the pen, the eager customer would begin to write, and only the color blue would show up. "Doesn't work, Doc," the customer would say disgustedly. "Oh, yes, it does," John would answer quickly. "Here, see it spells red, yellow and green." The customer would walk away shaking his head, "You won't do, Doc. You just won't do."

John was also right there joking with his own employees. When they complained of being very weary, John would firmly remind them, "It's not what you do on the job that makes you tired." If a customer asked for a horse and buggy, he would tell his workers to go to the attic to look for one, rather than to just say no. Healing was his first priority, however, be it laughter or medicine. That is why his customers kept coming back for "A Dose of Humor".

DRIVING LESSONS
Lynda Holmes

"If your wife wants to learn to drive, don't stand in her way."

--Stan Levenson

When I was a young girl in 1956, Mama begged Daddy to teach her to drive so that he wouldn't be run ragged taking us everywhere. As a result, Daddy agreed to give her driving lessons. After weeks of practice, under Daddy's supervision at the wheel of our black, 1951 Plymouth, Mama was driving well enough to get her driver's license. We had some memorable experiences as a result of Mama learning to drive.

One chore that Mama and I used the Plymouth to accomplish during my early years was getting to the bank. Back in those days, we had to go all the way into town to do our banking because we didn't have suburban services yet. Thus, Mama trained me to jump out of the car with the deposit slip, money envelope, and any other transactional paperwork, and run inside to take care of our banking needs. This plan eliminated the need to search for a never-available parking space around the town square in Decatur, Georgia.

I stood in line at the teller's window until my turn came, and then I stepped up to the window and laid my bounty on the counter.

"Hello, there, miss," the bank teller said. "How are you doing today?"

"Just fine, ma'am," I replied, as Mama had taught me to respond politely while I waited.

"O.K. Here's your receipt. Would you like a piece of candy, too?"

I nodded my head up and down for "Yes," said "Thank you," and ripped into the sucker. Cherry was my favorite flavor.

Outside the bank, I waited for the Plymouth to come back from around the square and pick me up. Thus, Mama and I completed our banking through teamwork. It was much like Bonnie and Clyde, except we didn't rob the bank or kill anyone before we made our getaway.

Mama's driving abilities also played a large part in saving the day for me on one particular occasion. I had a record player that played the old 78's (remember that we didn't have 8-track, cassette tapes, or CD's yet), and I could spend hours in my bedroom listening to my records and singing along with them.

A recording of "Little Red Riding Hood and the Wolf" was one of my favorites because of the wolf's scary growl when he talked to Red and Grandma. I hid under my bed when the wolf started growling, and I wouldn't come out until the record ended. Although this recording was totally frightening to me, I listened to it over and over again.

One Saturday, I had just come out from under the bed after listening to "Red Riding Hood," and I put on a recording of "Davy, Davy Crockett, King of the Wild Frontier." As I sang, I danced around the room, trying to emulate the dancing I had seen on television during "American Bandstand." I closed my eyes, imagining myself dancing on TV; this process caused me to lose my balance. I tripped over my own feet, falling down and bumping the back of my head hard on the bed post. I sat there a minute or two until the pain eased up a bit. Deciding that additional dancing practice would have to wait for another day, I walked into the living room and sat down on the floor to look at a *Little Golden Book*.

Before I could turn more than one page, Mama came rushing toward me screaming. She grabbed me up and ran with me out to the back steps, holding me in a hammerlock under one arm. Mama took hold of our mop, which was lying in its place across the railing and threw it down below. Daddy was pushing the lawn mower across the back yard at the time, so he couldn't hear anything over the noise of the mower's engine.

I will never forget the shocked look on his face as the mop hit him on the shoulder, and he looked up to see why the sky was raining mops that day. One look at Mama holding me under her arm while waving the other one wildly, he cut off the mower and came running up the back steps. Apparently, I was bleeding profusely from the back of the head. I remember Daddy grabbing me from Mama.

"Just go on and get the car keys and a towel and give her to me," Daddy instructed her. "I'll apply pressure to help stop up the bleeding on the way to the emergency room while you drive us there."

"I'll meet you at the car," Mama replied, as she ran off to find the car keys, not missing a beat.

We somehow made it into the Plymouth and away we went to the hospital. I lay in Daddy's lap as he pressed a towel firmly over my bleeding head. Mama drove us to the hospital safely. I remember feeling a profound sense of peace and calm from being near the two people who would always do their best to love me and care for me, no matter how challenging the circumstances: Mama and Daddy. We were a family.

2006 *Northeast Georgia Writers*: First Place, Inspirational Article

Evelyn, The Skeleton
Patsy C. Paget
(Skeleton in the Closet)

There's somebody special I want you to meet.
She's Evelyn, the skeleton with bony, long feet.
She lives in my closet up high on a shelf.
In a box, in the dark, she amuses herself.
She laughs and tells jokes with hosts of ghosts;
Shares secrets with witches and chats with cats.
Nestled with scarecrows and bats, she naps
As Digits, a spider, crawls over her lap.

She dreams of the time of year drawing near
When she and her comrades come down from their tier;
When they're out of the closet and onto the scene
As part of a season that's called Halloween.

They'll be joined by a jack-o-lantern named Glow,
Nocturne---an owl, and a windsock called Woooo.
Together they'll form a backdrop of spooks
For children in costume who laugh and shout, **"Boo"**!

1998 *Northeast Georgia Writers*: First Place, Assigned Subject

IN A PICKLE
Julianna Ramsey

Paula's oldest kid, Drew, loved dill pickles. He proclaimed them his favorite food and ate them as often as his mom would allow. He even asked for pickles in his scrambled eggs. The other kids came home from school and had cookies or a piece of fruit for a snack, but brother Drew had a pickle. Paula wondered if all that pickle eating wasn't the cause of her number one son's sour early morning disposition.

One morning he came into the kitchen with his usual groggy and sour little face; insisting that his mom make him a sliced dill pickle sandwich for his lunch box. She refused, explaining that by lunchtime it would have turned into a very soggy and distasteful mess. He refused to understand her reasoning and would not take no for an answer. The battle began; as every morning he harangued, whined, and argued with his mom for that pickle sandwich, while she remained adamantly against it.

At the breakfast table, this power struggle was the main topic of conversation. Drew's three younger brothers giggled and teased Drew about his weird request. Their friends had labeled their mom "the drill sergeant," as she was a strict disciplinarian. So no matter what, they all knew that eventually mom was going to be the winner of this struggle. They taunted Drew with, "You better stop arguing with mom before you lose your privileges." However, Drew loved being the center of attention and was clearly enjoying the fuss he was causing. As the oldest child, he had learned just how far he could go with his mom without incurring her total wrath.

Paula, busy each morning providing a nutritious, sit down breakfast for her brood, as well as packing their school lunches, got more and more aggravated with Drew, but held her temper at bay. No reason to lose her cool, she reasoned, over something so silly.

Paula's husband stayed out of the fray. When friends and family described Steve, the stereotype "strong and silent type" was often mentioned. A big strapping guy with a gentle personality, Steve was a great dad, very involved in his children's lives; teaching them by example. He hated confrontation and this forced Paula to dish out the discipline and the punishments.

Every morning, Steve sat quietly, sipped his coffee, and tried his best to concentrate on sports news in the paper, ignoring the pickle battle. After four consecutive mornings of listening to a whining son and looking at a scowling wife, Steve finally lost his patience. He got up and without a word, as his children watched, went up behind Paula, who was cooking oatmeal, and put his arms around her. He nuzzled her cheek and murmured assertively, but ever so softly in her ear, "Hon, give Drew a pickle sandwich."

I was enjoying a cup of after dinner coffee at Steve and Paula's, as Paula related this little family story to me. I asked, "So, did you?" "Yes, I took Steve's advice. I put *lots* of slices of pickle in that sandwich." "Well, what happened?" I asked. Steve glanced at Paula, then turned to me and answered, with a sly little grin, "He never asked for another pickle sandwich."

THE CHANGE-MAKER
Norval P. Caples

He began showing up daily in the main hallway, taking a position near the entrance of the large general hospital.

Tall, almost gaunt, he stood untiring and erect, greeting passersby with a smile and a kindly twinkle in his eye. Well beyond retirement age, this graying but still vigorous man quickly became a favorite among the fifteen hundred visitors and hospital workers who passed by him daily.

His activities did not go unnoticed; the hospital administrators were quick to see his potential and hired him to do what he was already doing. He was furnished a chair and a cash box from which to dispense change to the throngs of visitors and employees seeking coins to use in the pay telephones, and the newspaper and soft drink vending machines lining the busy hallway.

Although the change-maker quickly learned to identify hundreds of people who passed by his station daily, few knew very much about him. Quite talkative, he was an even better listener and skillfully diverted attention from himself.

With his friendly manner and easy approachability, he frequently had more than he could handle in assisting grieving or bewildered visitors who sought him out for a wide variety of concerns. Sometimes his clear and oft repeated directions would not be grasped; then the change-maker would leave his chair to accompany a grateful visitor to his destination.

But nothing goes on forever except taxes, and too soon, it seemed, the change-maker was gone too. His exit was sudden; literally overnight he stopped showing up at his hallway station. The greetings and the cheerful banter were gone, as was the bustle of activity that always seemed to surround him. The chair and the cash box, unneeded now, were carried away.

A mildly critical "Letter to the Editor" had appeared in *The Times*. The writer had visited the hospital, witnessed the hallway activity and was writing to protest the change-maker's position as trivial and meaningless in a large, bustling—state of the art—general hospital.

The thought had just never entered anyone's mind before then that his services were superfluous and should be discontinued. But the hospital staff, patients and visitors alike, missed the change-maker right away, and they still do.

Lost Dream
Patsy C. Paget

A lady turned the calendar to the month of December. She picked up a book and began reading to her new little son.

"Twas the night before Christmas when all through the house---"

As she read, the smells of December seemed to rise from the page. She became entranced. The familiar scent of red holly candles sweetened the air. She closed her eyes, breathed deeply, and reeled with the fragrance of pine garlands on the mantle. No longer a grown-up lady with a baby, she was a child again, reliving a Christmas of long ago. She imagined the aroma of her mother's cookies baking in the oven. The essence of her beautiful cedar Christmas tree filled the room. The wonder of Santa Claus returned, and she thought of the red bicycle he would soon place beneath that tree.

The little girl, dreaming of her favorite season, could not know of the mean, hateful child who would soon destroy her beautiful Christmas dream.

"Don't say that! There is a Santa Claus! The devil will get you for not telling the truth!" she cried.

"Ha, Ha!" he taunted. "You're a baby. You still believe in Santa Claus. There is no Santa. Your mother and daddy bring your toys." He began to chant, "You are a baby. You think there's a Santa Claus."

"No! I'm not a baby! Santa Claus is real. I'll tell my Mother what you said. She will tell your mother and your mother will punish you for telling lies."

The girl could not run fast enough. Her heart was pounding and she felt hot. She had to get to her mother. Her mother would tell her that Santa is real; that he would come as he had always done. He had elves and reindeer. He was jolly and bright. He would put her toys underneath the tree; read her note; eat her cookies; return to his sleigh and dash away! Mother would tell her not to pay attention to that evil boy.

The mother listened to her little girl, took her into her arms, and gently explained the myth of Santa Claus. No reading of "Yes, Virginia, there is a Santa Claus," could console the heartbroken child. She had lost her dream. Christmas would never be the same. She cried and cried.

The grown-up lady, summoned to the present by the cooing of the baby in her arms, wiped a tear from her cheek, placed a kiss on the baby's head, and continued her reading---

"but I heard him exclaim as he drove out of sight,
   'Merry Christmas to all and to all a goodnight!'"

1997 *Northeast Georgia Writers*: First Place, Fiction

LIFE WITHOUT JURGEN
Kate McConnon

The day is empty
But I'll make it full
The kitchen echoes quiet
And I don't hear your firm step or
Feel the scent of your aftershave
We don't butter our toast and chat
I butter my toast and listen to the radio
Or watch the TV
Going about my usual chores-check the plants
Empty the dishwasher
Check the calls I need to return
Ah- and plan for dinner….
But you won't be here
I can have the baked beans you never liked.
I stand tall and put my shoulders back-
I can do this
I must
Life demands my participation
The kids will worry
They try to cushion my day with such love and care
But then I see your merry eyes in a picture on the fridge
Or a familiar note sounds
Or a special word is said
And I dissolve
And melt
And falter
With missing you forever more.

2005 *Northeast Georgia Writers:* Award for Poetry

WHEN I LOOK AT YOU . . .
Harriet Woodcock

Several years ago, I had the privilege of working in the Alzheimer's wing of an assisted living home. I say privilege, because it gave me the opportunity to somehow reach a mind that is lost to doubt and uncertainty.

When I first became Emily Dunlap's companion, there were only traces of memory lapses beginning to rear their doubting heads. Both of us, being senior citizens, had great times talking about old times. Our families had been intertwined throughout the years, and memories of shared experiences were numerous between us.

For some reason, remembering incidences from long ago are much easier for older folks than recalling what they had for lunch that day. Emily had a background of music similar to mine, and glorious recollections of our opera experiences were happy occasions.

Emily had sung arias in operas, while I played an instrument in the accompanying orchestra. Photographic pictures, found in the mind's eye, can easily span any given time or place.

There were occasions when Emily would ask to go for a ride. She always wanted to go by the college with which her family had been connected for years. Her father was president of the institution at one time, and Emily had many stories to tell about that phase of her life.

Sometimes, however, the past got mixed up with the present, and my friend would want to stop and go in the house that once belonged to her parents. "I wish to see my Mother and Father," she would say with urgency. Gathering up all of my courage, I would reply, "But Emily, they have long ago passed away." This statement was always followed by a frown and a sigh. And yet, Emily seemed to accept this fact from me, and would readily go on to another subject. Thank goodness, God shifts the forgetful mind gently from one subject to another.

Sometimes, when we got back to the home, Emily would not recognize the building or even her own room. Fretful moments would occur, and she would say mournfully, "I want to go home." Firmly, I would look into her eyes and say, "But you are home. This is your home, Emily." A blank stare made me realize that Emily did not associate the care home as her living place, but she seemed reconciled to take the statement as a word of truth from her friend.

There were moments of clearness when she would ask me to phone some members of her family. Oftentimes, she could not remember what they did, or when she had last seen them. But just to hear their voices seemed to satisfy her. In return, the family had the great satisfaction of knowing that their relative was well taken care of, with prepared meals and constant companions. There were even good times when her loved ones came for frequent visits, or to take her out to dinner.

The happiest times for her seemed to be when planned activities at the institution provided musical entertainment. Emily would join in heartily with the rest of the singers. It became more and more amazing to me that although she could no longer carry on an intelligent conversation, she could remember every word of the music that was sung.

As time went on, Emily became more unsteady on her feet, and a cane did not provide enough stabilization. Her friends and relatives hated to see her succumb to a walker, but we all realized that this was to be the best solution. Even with the falls, the frustrations and setbacks that my ward experienced, she always kept a bright, cheerful smile upon her face. That beautiful look carried all of her caregivers through the rough times.

And as for me, there was that special day when Emily turned to me with a statement of profound wisdom that put even my own life back on track. Looking me straight in the eye, she professed, "When I look at you, I know who I am."

Thank you, Emily.

Requiem for a Matriarch
Marsha Hopkins

Dark filings to a magnet –
We came.
The whole town it seemed,
Quietly we walked
From blocks away –
Pulled together to honor our community matriarch –
To her church of grey stone and honeyed wood –
Of towered bells that punctuate the hours of our days.
She and her church, both strong and stately and so
Central to the life we know here.
All pews plus more chairs filled
And many figures stood silently in the wings.
Music of Eastertide filled the air as choir members from
Different denominations sang together –
And slanted sunrays bathed the cross.
Then all were invited to bow and share Communion.
Ninety years she had on earth –
Fifty plus of those she spent in this place
Welcoming all with her gracious hospitality –
Always beautifying, uplifting, praying,
And reaching out –
Making life better for those in need. Serving others.
Never hurried. Always taking time to care.
Savoring life –
One precious moment –
One individual person – At a time.

In memory of Jane Eve Wilheit, 1916–2007

Pictures on the Journey

From the Balcony
Mary Ellen Collier

Sunset at Lake Lanier

Night is slowly closing over Lake Lanier.
The trees look so mystical
with the mist casting a halo over them.
Two small boats are gliding by like
beautiful swans.
There is one opening in the magnificent sky
that is still a brilliant white.
It may be where you step into heaven.

The sunset has been a fireball.
Now it is lowered, and there are delicate
little clouds floating across it.
As this wonder sinks deeper and deeper
into the water,
it takes on a pink glow
which reflects all over the lake.

What a glorious painting God
has given us this evening.
The serenity that surrounds
the scene is a prayer of thanks.
How very difficult it would
be to duplicate this beauty
anywhere else in the world.

Free verse poetry published by *Lakeside News*, Fall Issue, 1997

THE KEEPER
Ruthanna Bass

Moss and rock line the neatly swept room
The furniture consists of a tree stump or two
Bending closer I find a little straw broom
And tea cups made from walnut hulls
A tin dish, a fork and some spoons.
A trickle of a stream runs just below
As the dark invades the forest fills with gloom
The last rays of sunshine sprinkle this space
How lucky I am to have found this place
In leaving I vow to return very soon
And have tea with the keeper
Of this lovely, little room.

GREEN STREET
Ruthanna Bass

Green Street winds
Like a ribbon through time
Stately white mansions
Majestically pose
Waiting for the next generation
To snap the picture
In their minds' eye
Saved to the gallery
Virtually unchanged
But for the occupants
Who work and rest
In a place where grace
Refuses to die.

Pages in a Book
Barbara H. Harper

I open the diary and read. The pages contain no words. They are far from empty - these leaves from the BOOK OF MY LIFE. I turn the pages slowly and watch them fill with physical images and personalities and ideas. How can I extract only one person? If one insists on competing for the title of "Person who has influenced my life;" then that one wins – for the moment.

Each of these pages is a "Section" of my life. The memories of the more special persons in that "Section" audition for that person to be written about as a person who influenced my life.

A page comes alive with color! Two persons stand out on this page. One was a young woman of my own age of 20 years. We were so close she almost did "walk in my shoes" and I in hers. The other was a young man I remember with love; though at the time nothing was right for us to walk together in any shoes.

I tell myself to "Put the book back on the shelf."

I don't. I am a compulsive reader.

I have already made the mistake made by others before me. I "flipped through" the Mother and Father pages. It was these two who helped me develop the skill of knowing how to appreciate any person I have met or will meet.

I read the Wife page. My husband was a very positive man! One page can not reveal the indelibleness of his effect on me and on others!

The next page nudges my finger urging, "Turn!" Here I was the Mother. Such rewarding experiences! Do I find here a person who influenced my life? I do! Four of them!

The book has more pages. In the Section bearing the title "After the Death of My Husband" I see materialize some new "old friends" who wrote themselves in my heart. My sisters proved also to be good friends. Two special counselors emerge, one in Law Matters and one in Spiritual Matters. These became caring friends. I was surprised and delighted to find again another friend with whom I have shared the closeness of "Let's walk each in the other's shoes."

The last page is still being written – a good, long page, I hope.

So – I have been influenced by all those I have loved and who have loved me. I have sifted results. I have made choices. I have accepted as part of my thinking, my beliefs, my being, influences from each of many persons. Not one of them had magical powers to force nor used hypnotism. They were and I was and I became.

In the end, a person, the person, who influenced my life for good or bad was – Me.

2007 Northeast Georgia Writers: Second Place, Assigned Subject

PURPLE FLOWERS
Mary Ellen Collier

When you left us, it was spring.
Purple little flowers abounded everywhere.
You know how you always loved flowers,
And they were there for you waving a sweet good-bye.

Purple was always your color.
It is a color of royalty.
To me, and many others,
You were a queen among the earthly flowers.

A year has passed.
The purple flowers are back.
They are a touch of your queenly presence
Gracing us once again.

I miss you, Mom, so much,
But how comforting to know your quiet beauty
Surrounds us still.
I only have to look around me to feel your caring touch.

2001 *Northeast Georgia Writers*: First Place, Free Verse Poetry

THE DAY MY SON BECAME A MARINE
Gloria Cassity Stargel

What time I am afraid, I will trust in thee.
Psalm 56:3 (KJV)

"Bye, Mom," Rick said as he planted a kiss on my cheek and gave me one last firm hug.

"Bye, Son," I managed, then watched him fold his broad-shouldered, six-foot frame into his friend's tiny, green sports car. *I will not cry,* I told myself. *Not until he's out of sight.*

I think I had dreaded this day ever since he was born—this day when our last child would leave home. That he should be going into military service caused even more gnawing fear.

He wouldn't let me go see him off at the airport. "No emotional scenes, please." *I'll stay busy,* I told myself. *Try not to think.* No matter. My eyes kept glancing at the clock. Was it time yet for Flight 304? At the appointed hour, I could stand it no longer.

Running by the closet, I grabbed my heavy coat and hurried out into the backyard. We're only 50 miles from Atlanta International. Maybe I can see his plane from here. I realized I probably couldn't. But I just had to try. I yearned for one more glimpse, even though from 20,000 feet.

I raced down the hill behind the house to a large clearing with a view of the sky in all directions. I barely noticed the near-perfect weather of an autumn afternoon. Instead I saw the old oak tree farther down in the backyard, looking forlorn, stripped now of its leaves.

I knew how the tree felt. A part of my life had just ended as I said good-bye to twenty-two years of joy. My chest hurt so from the burden, I wondered if perhaps the heart *does* break at times. *Where have the years gone?* I wondered. *Wasn't it just yesterday that we brought the blue bundle home from the hospital? Now he's going off to become a Marine Corps officer with all that implies.*

Yet, I kept seeing him as a curly-haired toddler with huge brown eyes shining in a cherubic face, all love and innocence. *By training him to fight, will they destroy all the tenderness that I've nurtured?*

Anyway, it's not fair, I grumbled. I wanted him to grow up to be independent, and I'm proud of his willingness to serve his country. *Still, you do a good job as a parent and you put yourself right out of business.*

Tortured with these conflicting sentiments, I shrank from this day. Now it had arrived and I stood searching the sky. Only a few clouds floated in the huge expanse. I clutched my coat tighter. Dear Jesus, help me, I sobbed, grasping for the comfort I had *learned to expect from my faith. Take away this awful pain.*

The distant drone of a jet engine broke my reverie. There it is! That must be it! Rick's plane. It's climbing and heading north.

Then, just as suddenly as it appeared, it slid into the heavens, out of sight. He was out there alone somewhere...

I stared at the vacated space in the sky. *Good-bye, Son. Good-bye.*

Reluctantly I trudged back into the house, pleading, *Dear God, You tell us in your Word to cast all our cares upon you because You care for us*. So, Lord, here, I give You my burden. I can't carry it alone.*

But after I gave God my burden, I took it right back. I forgot all about the message in the great old hymn "Take your burden to the Lord and leave it there."

Instead, the next day I was back in the grips of self-pity. I avoided Rick's room with the quiet radio workbench and the basement with his weights stacked neatly in the corner. It was more than pain of separation. I sensed that Rick could never be the same; and my grief for that loss was wrenching, tearing.

Late that day, I stood at the kitchen window, gazing out at another afternoon sky, lost in memories. Finally my eyes again focused on the old oak tree in the backyard. With its bare branches it looked as sad as I felt.

But this time I saw something I hadn't seen before. Those bare branches reached expectantly upward, confident of new life next spring. They presented a picture of faith, of trust. I felt a surge of hope, for it was as if God Himself had shown me that picture when I needed it most. Surely I had known that I could trust my son to God. And that I could trust God to heal my hurt. Had I failed to reach up to him, in trust?

Forgive me, Lord, I prayed as I bowed my head and my heart before him. *Teach me, once more, to trust you in all things.*

A calmness filled my consciousness as I gradually yielded to our Lord's tender care. Finally I could add the close to my prayer. *Now, God, I turn Rick over to You. I guess, really, You had him all the time, didn't You? Thank you, Father, for those beautiful twenty-two years.*

Once again I studied the old oak tree down the hill. Now we had even more in common, that old tree and me. For I, too, reached expectantly upward and my burden felt strangely lightened. And though the tears were still in my eyes, I knew that this, too, would pass. That tomorrow—or the next tomorrow—I would smile again.

At last, across the miles, I whispered my benediction: "Good-bye, my son. Goodbye. May God, who loves you, hold you in the palm of his hand."

And I knew now that He would. Yes, God would take care of Rick. And me.

I had learned—once again—that faith means trust.

*1Peter 5:7 (KJV)

Published in *Chicken Soup for the Mother/Son Soul, Standard, Advocate, Evangel and Power for Living* Magazines

THE CABIN
Diana Wildman

(Beginning page of a novel)

    The large liquid moon rose above the forest, dripping an eerie light about the lonely cabin. Tall trees, barren specters now in the dead of winter, their skeleton-like limbs entwined, stand guard around the clearing where their shadows sway and contort in a silent ghost dance.

    Now and then a limb leaves the circle to scrape its long bony fingers across the cold glass of the cabin windows, breaking the unearthly silence. But there is no one to hear. The cabin is empty now, its once clean-swept floors rotting, its porch, where roses used to climb, strangled now by corpulent vines, and its lone occupant remembered solely by a headstone which marks the grave in the clearing. —Marthae Anderson 1812—

BLUE HERON
Leona Peffly Martin

Lazily rising from the creek at my approach,
The blue heron flapped its wings and flew upstream.
I had only caught a glimpse of it before
As I startled it from its favored feeding ground
Replete with minnows, snakes, frogs and crawdads.

Sometimes I'd see the kingfisher skimming by,
Close to the water, chattering as it went,
But the heron was always quiet like a shadow
That I sensed more than saw as it flew away
Through the soft gray mist of morning.

This time it rose deliberately from the water,
Its broad wings moving so slowly as it lifted
To fly without fear from my intrusion.
Its color seemed more vivid as I watched it.
Before I had thought it was more gray than blue.

What a picture to put away in memory,
The blue heron flying up the creek,
Flapping its wide wings lazily as it went,
With its own purpose, away from me
To seek seclusion for its morning hunt.

Previously published: *In the Woodland and other poems by Leona Peffly Martin,* 2000 (a self-published chapbook), and *A Continuing Quest, poems 1945 – 2005* by Leona Peffly Martin, 2005, iUniverse, Inc.

HAVEN
Leona Peffly Martin

Our house sits on a hill;
Below us is the creek.
The trees enclose our space;
We have no need to seek
Beyond our little world
For beauty or for peace.
All we need is here,
Where we have found surcease.

The jangling of the world
Is muffled by the trees,
Except for faintest echoes
Carried on the breeze.
No longer do we scramble
And hope that we can find
The answers to our questions,
Tranquility of mind.

We feel the living Spirit
And breathe Him with the air.
We sense in His creation
The measure of His care.
We need no church to worship,
No altar for our prayer.
The earth is our cathedral:
Our God is everywhere.

2005 *Northeast Georgia Writers*: Second Place, Poetry
Previously Published: *A Continuing Quest, Poems 1945-2005*
by Leona Peffly Martin (2005), iUniverse, Inc.

HONORED WOMAN
Mary Ellen Collier

The Cherokees were valiantly brave
As they left their land,
Led from their Godly serenity
By the White Man.

Honored Woman, when you feel the
Sweet caress of the wind - -
Know it is your ancestors speaking,
"Never let your heart bend."

Oh, how the winds blow down through the years
Some gentle - - some strong
Changing man's course as
He travels along.

Your ancestors heard the force of the winds,
As they proudly trudged forward into the unknown,
Wondering if their wounded hearts
Would ever mend.

Too much – too much
Was taken away,
But the magnificent Spirit
Remains with us this very day.

They sent down to you from that rugged trail
Strength, gentleness and a prideful heart,
Which you shared with your friends
From the very start.

As you celebrate your great journey today,
The winds will allow you to carry your Cherokee Spirit
To others who are on their trail
Of Life's Way.

FAMILIES
Elouise Whitten

December 1, 2001
Happy Birthday Dear Courtney,

Now that you are 12, I will fulfill this year, a promise I made to you in a letter when you were born, about getting all the information about the several families you were born into. Over the past twelve years I have compiled as much history of our families as I can. I know most about your grandfather Richard's family—the Whitten family from your mother, Lisa's side, into which I married. We will have to research more about your grandmother, Donna's family and possibly on your father, Todd Crawford's family. It will be our Genealogy Project of researching, recording and sharing the Whitten, Brown and Crawford family records as far as we can. I don't even know your dad's mother's maiden name yet. From the day you receive this several-generational record I have collected, I'm asking you to take over and preserve it for the generations that follow you.

To you on this 12th birthday, I give the known past record and the work of recording any future stories for your family records. I will still assist you.

It is sad that so many families do not keep records. I have precious little about my mother's maternal Angevine family and her paternal Lake family. I remember that great-grandfather Angevine was a Heron Indian and great-grandmother Angevine's family came from France. I don't know her maiden name. I have less about my dad's paternal Rentfro family and I don't have a record of my father's mother's maiden name either. Her name was Anna. She died when Dad was about three when his baby sister, Bernice, was born. There were five boys and two girls in his family. The oldest, Aunt Mary, cared for the baby and all her brothers. She was my favorite of Dad's family. She and I both became cosmetologists and owned our own shops. She was dead years before I opened my business. I will continue to search the web sites and record libraries and add stories.

Your great-grandfather and my husband, Doyle Chadwick Whitten (Barney), is fortunate to have three cousins who gathered a fair bit of information and pictures of their Whitten Family's past generations back to the war of 1812. I went to the National Records Library in Atlanta, GA. and rechecked their accuracy. I have also written what I could gather about both his mother's paternal Smith family and her maternal family. I don't have either of her names. It is sad, really sad.

I will add pictures to the book I compile for you. Together, we will interview your father, Todd's family in 2002, and set the Crawford family record down in black and white for you to continue. I don't know Todd's mother's maiden name but with your father's knowledge of the computer and Internet you two should have enjoyable hours together. You are growing up into a fine young woman and as you look back on your life, you will appreciate this record keeping more and more – so will all those who follow you.

Your mother, Lisa, is the oldest of my eleven grandchildren. You are the oldest of my eleven great-grandchildren. You are both special to me. She and your grandmother, Donna, will furnish information about her Brown family.

God will add more to our family through the years and some will leave us. Always remember that every individual is special, each in his or her own way. That is what makes life and their stories so interesting. God has a wonderful plan for each person and it is our privilege to ASK Him what that plan is so that we will go about life doing the best we can do to make our lives count in a significant way of honoring Him and helping others. It is a work we should wake up to each day – to all the wonder and surprise each day brings. Recording your journey in a journal will help you eventually write the story of your life and share it with the families you are born into. Add your budding talent as an artist to your writing and we will all await the outcome. Art and writing are both noble works.

We love you Precious One.
    Love, Great Granny (GG)

2002 *Northeast Georgia Writers*: First Place Award, Special Category

AFRICAN MARKET DAY
Kate McConnon

It was a market day. Four of us were going to visit Mushin Market in Lagos, Nigeria. Our ostensible "purpose" was a kitten for my friend, Val. Irene, my young neighbor and relatively new arrival to Lagos had gotten a kitten at this market and Val decided she wanted one too. Irene, our intrepid leader for this mission, came down to my flat in a gray fleece bra sports top with a large baggy sweater. Inwardly I groaned, not a good outfit for an oyebo (foreigner) woman to wear to a market. Brit, a young Peace Corps volunteer was staying overnight at my house and leaving Nigeria for Eden Prairie, Minnesota the next day. She had lost sixty pounds in Nigeria from an undiagnosed malady which seemed to be ravaging her lungs. She was a game addition to our expedition on her last day.

Val and Sam, her reliable and amiable Ghanaian driver, picked us up. Sam didn't exactly know where Mushin Market was (no one is ever quite sure where anything is in the sprawling Lagos proper) but he knew the general direction and he assured us he would get us there.

Two hours later driving across traffic-laden bridges and through a labyrinth of small and winding streets, Sam did find the endless market that must have had at least fifty inlets and egresses. Irene, of course had no idea which entrance was the "kitten" entrance so Sam pulled over and we disembarked and strode authoritatively into the world of Mushin Market. After striding what seemed like several city blocks through narrow teeming passages we realized we needed an idea of where we were going and a guide to get us out of this place when we were finished. The air in the murkily lit market was still and dark and scorching hot, filled with the smells of spices, sewage, and humanity all cramped and crowded and jammed into this nether world. We asked at a stall selling oil and various condiments where we could find a kitten. The proprietors of this space were a crinkly older woman and her assistant, a regal young woman with arching cheekbones in a brilliant pink native outfit and matching headdress. We didn't know the Yoruba (one of many languages in Nigeria) word for kitten so we did a lot of obnoxious meowing and finally the Pink One took off with assertive strides toward the kittens (we hoped), all of us in fast-paced tow.

Mushin Market is a market for Lagos natives, not foreigners hoping to find a beautiful basket or a piece of cloth. It is a place to buy food, buttons, car parts, plastic containers, light bulbs, shoes, books, paper, the stuff of everyday life. Our presence there was an event and as the heat mounted in our never-ending striding, Irene took her sweater off and her pale midriff seemed liked a beacon for dark eyes to stare and wonder at these four strange white oyeboes.

Occasionally, the Pink One who was very charming and moved on fleet-footed feet would be verbally questioned in Yoruba as to who, what, and where we were going and she would reply as we whisked on our way, occasioning a chortling laugh or a guffaw. We were fording sewage streams, squeezing against overflowing merchandise and ducking oncoming pedestrians and in the wider areas, cars as we traversed this mysterious dark world of commerce. Finally we stopped. We were surrounded by a penned, smelly variety of miserable creatures in wire cages, makeshift baskets, squawking and howling. The eager and ever alert hawker-owners were watching every nuance of our reactions. A woman came forward with a small basket and raised the lid to reveal a scrawny and utterly undesirable full grown cat. We tried to signal that we wanted a small one in all manner of hand gestures. Eventually she shrugged with disgust and moved on--no sale and who knows what these foolish oyeboes want anyway?

The Pink One, although disappointed she did not find us what we wanted, knew she had scoured the market and the fault was not hers. She was tall and erect and elegant as she led us out of the myriad dark turns into the blistering sun once again and miraculously not far from Sam who had been patiently waiting for us. We gave her gracious thanks for her efforts and pressed some naira (money) into her calloused palm because she had given us her time which was money to her. She smiled and disappeared back to her stall and her life.

We all folded into the car with relief and certain hilarity after our arduous foray. What must they think? What were we thinking? Why do we want a kitten from the progenitors such as that scrawny cat anyway?

The air conditioning reached full tilt and I secretly thought of the utter reek of Irene's apartment since her cat had joined her household. A fact that could be attributed to her total lack of smell which she confessed to me one day. A curse in many places perhaps but not in the bowels of Lagos, Nigeria and certainly not Mushin Market. Val would try another day and eventually land a kitten.

For us that day it was an adventure into another world that was novel and strange. But for the lovely and proud Pink One it was her life and livelihood. It made us all appreciate that we did not have to traverse such difficulties to secure even the most mundane stuff of life. We all remember the regal Pink One in the midst of it all, moving with such elegance and grace. When I hear of a riot in Africa I think of scenes like Mushin Market so primal, so teeming with life, fraught with a violent fragility and vigor that is so precarious. So far removed from the wide aisles of Publix, but so burned into my memory.

TALKING HANDS
Ruthanna Bass

Worn, spotted, beautiful hands
Endlessly expressing woeful thoughts
On an island where she is stranded
Waging a battle for so long fought
Don't you know I understand?
Each and every forlorn thought
Passes from a fertile land
Into younger, waiting hands.

FLYING HIGH
Lynda Holmes

              Kite
           K i te Kite
         Kite kite kite
       Kite kite kite kite
         Kite kite kite
           Kite kite
             Kite
              w
              i
             n
             d
            t
           a
          k
         e
       s
      i
     t
high high!
Hold on tight!

Author Index

Bass, Ruthanna 69, 80
Baumgardner, Elizabeth 14, 20
Brady, Samantha 15, 42, 46
Caples, Norval P. 45, 47, 61
Clark, Brenda 26, 33
Collier, Mary Ellen 68, 71, 76
Ellett, Margaret Stout 51, 52, 53
Emerson, Blanche Buchanan 4, 16, 21
Harper, Barbara H. 34, 35, 70
Harris, Laura Leigh 2, 5, 44
Harris-Mallinson, Rosemary 8, 9, 28
Holmes, Lynda 24, 57, 81
Hopkins, Marsha 7, 49, 66
Marlow, Julie 29, 46
Martin, Leona Peffly 31, 74, 75
McConnon, Kate 41, 63, 79
Paget, Patsy C. 50, 59, 62
Ramsey, Julianna 17, 25, 60
Stargel, Gloria Cassity 12, 39, 72
Whitten, Elouise 13, 37, 77
Wildman, Diana 18, 36, 74
Woodcock, Harriet 18, 56, 64